INSTITUTIONAL ETHNOGRAPHY

INSTITUTIONAL ETHNOGRAPHY

A Theory of Practice for Writing Studies Researchers

MICHELLE LAFRANCE

UTAH STATE UNIVERSITY PRESS
Logan

Published by Utah State University Press
An imprint of University Press of Colorado
245 Century Circle, Suite 202
Louisville, Colorado 80027

Printed in the United States of America

The University Press of Colorado is a proud member of the Association of University Presses.

The University Press of Colorado is a cooperative publishing enterprise supported, in part, by Adams State University, Colorado State University, Fort Lewis College, Metropolitan State University of Denver, University of Colorado, University of Northern Colorado, Utah State University, and Western State Colorado University.

∞ This paper meets the requirements of the ANSI/NISO Z39.48–1992 (Permanence of Paper).

ISBN: 978-1-60732-866-7 (paperback)
ISBN: 978-1-60732-867-4 (ebook)
DOI: https://doi.org/10.7330/9781607328674

Library of Congress Cataloging-in-Publication Data

Names: LaFrance, Michelle, author.
Title: Institutional ethnography : a theory of practice for writing studies researchers / Michelle LaFrance.
Description: Logan : Utah State University Press, [2018] | Includes bibliographical references and index.
Identifiers: LCCN 2019007030 | ISBN 9781607328667 (pbk.) | ISBN 9781607328674 (ebook)
Subjects: LCSH: English language—Rhetoric—Study and teaching (Higher)—Research—Methodology. | Academic writing—Study and teaching (Higher)—Research—Methodology. | Writing centers—Sociological aspects. | Universities and colleges—Sociological aspects.
Classification: LCC PE1404 .L266 2018 | DDC 808/.042072—dc23
LC record available at https://lccn.loc.gov/2019007030

Cover illustration, “Symmetrical image of brutalist building in Cologne, Germany,” © frederikloewer/Shutterstock.com

To Dan Soloff and Dylan, mentors and good friends
May the Summer Lands be sweet

CONTENTS

FOREWORD

Tony Scott

Composition and rhetoric is still an applied field, and much of the scholarship that circulates in scholarly forums continues to be produced with at least an implicit premise that it will influence pedagogical practice and hence student learning. However, while the premise of scholarly influence on practice continues to be an important rationale sustaining the production of scholarship in the academic discipline, important questions surrounding the degree of actual influence of scholarship on practice remain very much open. Most scholarship is produced by tenure-line faculty in institutions that support research, but the great majority of postsecondary writing courses are not taught by teachers who are active scholars in composition and rhetoric. So who assumes responsibility for bringing practices into dialogue with scholarship, and what socio-material infrastructures facilitate it? Likewise, what ideas, agencies, and imperatives other than scholarship in composition and rhetoric influence how writing is conceived and taught, and how are they negotiated within particular environments? How, qualitatively, do ideas about writing and writing education manifest in the actual activities of teachers, students, and the educational ecologies they encounter and create?

Through the three studies brought together in this important book, Michelle LaFrance models a methodology that can help teachers, scholars, and administrators better understand how ideas about writing emerge and are negotiated among those who are doing the *work*—and LaFrance uses the term *work* in a very deliberate way—in complex institutional settings.

LaFrance locates ideas about composition work within the bureaucratic practices, disciplinary constructs, texts, and interpersonal relationships that define everyday institutional life in higher education. The methodology she uses, institutional ethnography, is within the traditions of cultural materialism, and the studies here depict composition work at its

DOI: 10.7330/9781607328674.c000a

most granular level of activity. Ideas about writing are material and distributed, and theory is an evolving, relational process that emerges within institutional ecologies that include syllabi, websites, course goals and mission statements, correspondence among faculty and administrative units, comments on students' papers, and all of the socio-material activities that produce writing education in institutional settings. The work of writing application and the work of writing theory is mediated within institutional processes. For instance, in one of the studies presented here, the institutional status of writing center administrators, along with the "boss texts" of the bureaucracies within which they work—position descriptions, annual review templates, and similar elements—are shown to have a significant effect on how writing center administrators do their work. "Staff" and "faculty" are perceived and reviewed differently, and this shapes their agencies and affordances—including the flexibility they have to interpret their work in relation to scholarship.

Because it offers researchers and teachers a way to understand composition as cultural material work, this book could not be more timely. We need conceptual frames that can help professional writing educators better respond to the actually existing environments of composition work and understand how those environments relate to circulating theories of curricula and pedagogy. As other recent research makes apparent, the work of higher education is being rapidly transformed. The already unwieldy scales of basic and introductory writing education are being expanded through digital technologies and the creation of competitive global education markets within which the politics of language and economics are problematically intertwined (see Martins 2015). Of course, also part of the institutional scenes of writing education are the vexed labor relations through which it continues to be mediated in a time of austerity economics, as most of composition's teaching work at US institutions continues to be performed by teaching assistants and part-time and full-time contract workers whose status seems ever more precarious (Welch and Scott 2016). Just as I began drafting this preface, colleagues in the writing program at SUNY Stony Brook asked for help with circulating a petition calling on the president of the university to reverse a decision about writing faculty cuts and program restructuring. Twenty-two adjunct-instructors who worked in the writing program at Stony Brook were told in October that they will not have their contracts renewed for the upcoming semester (Liebson 2017). The teaching performed by the "non-renewed" faculty in the writing and rhetoric program at Stony Brook will now be covered by a cadre of non-tenure-line instructors from other departments, including history, Asian American studies, pharmacology, and geology. Increases in class sizes are also planned. The non-renewed teachers in the writing program are left to find other work, facing a sudden and unanticipated loss of healthcare coverage and income with the normal life pressures of childcare costs, mortgages, student loan debt, and other expenses in the balance. Meanwhile, the writing program, which was not consulted about the cuts prior to the announcement, is left to adapt to the new reality of courses taught by faculty who were not hired to teach writing, have little or no scholarly or experiential background in teaching writing, and likely don't have any research or intellectual interests in writing education.

This transformation of how the work of composition is done will have a substantial effect on teaching and learning at SUNY Stony Brook, and the cuts and restructuring there mirror similar actions across the country, as institutions are continually told to be more "entrepreneurial" and do more as state appropriations for higher education continue to shrink (Mitchell, Leachman, and Masterson 2016). I posted the Stony Brook petition to the Writing Program Administration listserv, and some people indicated that they would sign. Some also expressed exasperation in forms that were at once understandable and now very familiar. A few people pointed out that resistance in the field had devolved over the years from advocating more tenure-line positions, to advocating full-time non-tenure-line positions, to fighting for the continuance of designated adjunct positions. Some also noted that the SUNY Stony Brook actions and similar actions at other institutions highlighted the precarious status of expertise in writing education.

We express empathy, anger and frustration; we offer support; we share descriptions of similar circumstances at our own or other institutions. Certainly, at least some solace can be found in the solidarity of our colleagues. However, notable in the usual responses to the retrenchment, loss of professional authority, budget cuts, and similar factors that are now so normal in our profession is that they are considered *problems of labor and institutionality*: problems that might be addressed, if at all, through local activism or administrative acumen. This response substantiates an entrenched categorical distinction between the work of materially embedded teaching and administration—the sphere of economic and institutional practices and procedures—and the "scholarly," more spatially and temporally transcendent work of writing research. The distinction suggests that in a more ideal world, teaching and scholarship would be allowed to flourish without being negatively affected by economic and organizational "problems" and with minimal bureaucratic interference from institutions. Our responses to news like the impending changes at SUNY Stony Brook expose our still underdeveloped conceptual, disciplinary foundation for questions having to do with institutional work and professional change. Scholarship still tends to be disembedded from institutional life, losing its relevance to practice and limiting the scope of theory.

In this book, LaFrance encourages us to see not just *problems* in the work of writing education but *problematics* within the institutions in which formal writing education happens. A problematic, LaFrance writes, "is not necessarily a 'problem,' such as the issue of low pay per course for contingent faculty. A problematic may begin with such a problem, but it then recognizes and accounts for the situated, complex, and interconnected relations among people, their experiences, and their practices related to that problem" (39).

Researching the problematics of writing work through institutional ethnography can show the always emergent possibilities of curricula, as it depicts the instability of pedagogy as theory in practice. In another study presented in this book, LaFrance describes a gateway course in which TAs are tasked to work with "lead faculty" in literature courses with a writing component. As the courses develop, so also do gaps in people's understandings of what writing in the classes should look like and do and how writing should be taught and assessed. The narrative of the gateway courses created by descriptions and goals of the courses was countered by intractable on-the-ground counter-narratives, by the disruptive presence of actually existing and agentive bodies in places doing things, and by differences in status and orientations among the instructors.

LaFrance shows how pedagogy is continually emergent and adaptive: the outcome of situated negotiations that belie any externally composed theory. We have theories of relations carrying considerable authority in the scholarship that blur distinctions between people and our environments—for instance, in ambient theories of rhetoric and the concept of entanglement in mobility studies—but we don't have enough qualitative research that tracks how theory emerges as activity in the institutional environments within which we and our students actually work together on a daily basis engaged in acts of composing, meaning making, and knowing.

Work matters. In addition to being a *problem,* the replacement of writing teachers and the dramatic transformation of the writing program at Stony Brook should also be seen as a problematic, a starting point for inquiry into the types of questions that are such a vital part of what composition studies can contribute to postsecondary writing education as an actual practice.

Does it matter to postsecondary writing education what sorts of spaces teachers and students work in? Is it in classes on main or satellite campuses, classes with tables, classes with desks in rows, online classes mediated through varied types of interfaces? Does it matter that some of our students walk to class from on-campus housing while others drive or take public transportation from off campus? Does it matter that some students come to classes having just dropped off children at schools or daycare or will drive straight from class to work? How is writing education affected by gateway assessments of language and writing competencies and the tracking that often follows? How is it influenced by the working lives of teachers? Some writing teachers go in to work and stop by their own offices before heading to class. Others share offices with other teachers, or they work from shared space in large common areas. Many writing teachers will teach three or more other writing classes in a day. Some will walk out of undergraduate classes in which they are teachers and into graduate classes in which they are students. Many will teach classes in other departments or other institutions in a single day. Some teachers will have a great amount of agency over what and how they teach, and others will not. What follows in this book is an argument for why work matters, and emerging out of these qualitative details of embedded institutional life in composition work are not just problems of activism and administration but problematics that writing studies needs to subsume within its sphere of research if it is to be relevant to writing education in the coming years.

This book adds to other recent work that addresses in some way how ecologies of learning and political economy relate to pedagogy: work such as that found in chapters in *Economies of Writing* (edited by Bruce Horner, Brice Nordquist, and Susan Ryan); in a special issue of *College Composition and Communication* on political economy (Fall 2016); in David Martins's excellent collection, *Transnational Writing Program Administration* (2015); in *Ecologies of Writing Programs: Program Profiles in Context* (Mary Jo Reiff, Anis Bawarshi, Michelle Ballif, and Christian Weisser 2015); and in Bruce Horner's *Rewriting Composition: Terms of Exchange* (2016). Generally, in this scholarship, terms of labor in composition are certainly a social justice issue, but their effects aren't just contained within a justice and advocacy conversation. Precarious terms for teachers are part of a larger economic dynamic with far-reaching consequences for the institutional learning environments of postsecondary writing. In this work, economic issues arising in austerity composition broaden the scope of composition scholarship—from the digital infrastructures that more efficiently connect students with often underpaid and disenfranchised teachers, to the international outsourcing of assessment, to the continued substantiation of monolingualism as a means of making writing education more scalable and efficient, to the pressures to make individual programs entrepreneurial and revenue-generating. Just as in LaFrance's institutional research, in much of this work, a clear distinction between theorization about composition and doing the daily theory work of composition shrinks or collapses altogether.

More studies of institutional work can contribute to an understanding of how we might further collapse the differences between theories and practices. The assumption that all teaching, reading, and composing is theory-in-action is either explicit or implicit within, for instance, teaching for transfer, writing about writing, translingual and transnational pedagogies, ambient rhetorics, multimodal and genre-based pedagogy. All of these curricular philosophies share an emphasis on awareness of the immediate, material environments of composing and uptake. In these curricula, composing is an activity and a mode of relations among people and the learning environments people inhabit and create. Among the assumptions are that language is emergent and constantly iterated, not static or bounded but reinvented in actual instances of use; that composing and theories of composing are cultural, dynamic, distributed, and embodied; and that meaning is continually emergent and created through ongoing translation within socio-material environments. This book shows in an exciting way that composing theory is not just a commodity for scholars: it is something we all *do* in the world. It is *work.* As work, writing education is unstable, produced, social, individual, distributed, and material.

ACKNOWLEDGMENTS

No one writes alone, especially not anxious perfectionists. I could not have completed this project without the literal village of colleagues, friends, soulmates, and four-leggeds who cheered and supported, nudged, elbowed and harangued, listened, coached, gave soothing and critical feedback, and reminded me to breathe, nap, trust, pick my battles, put some battles back, go to yoga, and get back to work.

So, my list of thank yous is quite long.

Much gratitude to Gail Stygall, who put Dorothy Smith's work into my hands in the very early stages of my dissertation project, saying "maybe this will help." To John Webster, who taught me to be an administrator and offered impromptu lectures on rhetoric, institutional politics, what theory doesn't get right, and the importance of a good long stretch every night. To Dan Soloff who said "yes, you do belong in graduate school" way back when, and to Kathy Mork who said "yes, you still belong in graduate school" when it mattered most. You, my mentors, helped me to lay the foundation that has served me and my work these many years.

So many others! Many, many thanks, raised glasses, and chocolates to E. Shelley Reid. It would be nearly impossible to have found a more ideal reader. Shelley offered critical feedback that pushed this manuscript beyond mere competence into saying something of value to other researchers. Melissa Nicolas patiently allowed me to co-opt a "little" project we were working on and to take it in directions neither of us originally anticipated—a better collaborator, mentor, guide, or friend you simply will not find. To Steven J. Corbett for *all the things*—reading and re-reading, for dinners, for long walks, for always listening and coaching. To Dylan, Pixie, and Maddy for all things dog.

Many thanks as well to Tony Scott for agreeing to write the foreword.

Anicca Cox and Seth Kahn, my favorite sort of riff-raff, read *the whole thing* and offered invaluable feedback, encouragement, and activist fuel. Michelle Miley reminded me that the work we do is always about relationships, courage, and vision. Darci Thoune, Katherine O'Meara,

Jennifer Zinchuk, and Travis Grady helped me to think expansively about the audience(s) for this work and its value to the field. Mitzi Jones and Brandon Fralix, who always hold space for my unrelenting introversion, remind me to drink only the best booze and to laugh loudly and often, and have never once teased me because I didn't know Dollywood would be dry.

To Tom and Emily who steered the ship while I was in the thick of it—every WAC director should be blessed with such a dream team. This book was also supported by a semester of faculty research leave granted by George Mason University in my third year, a gift of time and head space for which I am very grateful.

To my family, Elaine and Fred LaFrance, Alana Anderson, and Laurel Gandarilla, for the support and killer Scrabble showdowns. (I'm sure it will not be long before "Jugiqueens" appears in the OED.) To my dearest friends: Laurie Thompson, for kitchen table chats and the sort of friendship that could endure thirty years. (I love you, Girl.) To Jay Vanover and Mason Davenport for hikes, open fires, and star watching. To Mark Long, Jason Steiber, and Dana Driscoll for their fellowship. To Seumas and Lance for helping me put Old Town to bed on more than one visit. To Rath for every single one of those encouraging and funny texts in the last two hard, hard weeks.

And finally, to Andrew, who reminded me as I was finishing the manuscript that perfect need not be the enemy of done and that there should always be time for really good bourbon, live music, and a walk by the river with the dogs.

Ring the bells that still can ring Forget your perfect offering There is a crack in everything That's how the light gets in.

—Leonard Cohen, "Anthem"

Introduction

TWENTY-FIRST-CENTURY EXIGENCIES

Materialist Methods for Writing Studies

> *Ethnography is subversive—it challenges the dominant positivist view of making knowledge. It demands attention to human subjectivity and allows for author-saturated reconstructions and examinations of a world; in fact, it is grounded by definition in phenomenological understandings of knowledge and meaning making. Equally, it is generative and creative because writing research ethnographies are overtly rhetorical; they are producing informed stories and arguments about the world.*
>
> —Wendy Bishop, "I-Witnessing in Composition: Turning Ethnographic Data into Narratives"

> *Institutional ethnography explores the organizing INSTITUTIONS as people participate in them and from their perspectives. People are the expert practitioners of their own lives, and the ethnographer's work is to learn from them, to assemble what is learned from different perspectives, and to investigate how their activities are coordinated. It aims to go beyond what people know to find out how what they are doing is connected with other's doings in ways they cannot see. The idea is to MAP the institutional aspects of the RULING RELATIONS so that people can expand their own knowledge of their everyday worlds by being able to see how what they are doing is coordinated with other's doings elsewhere and elsewhen.*
>
> —Dorothy Smith, *Institutional Ethnography: A Sociology for People*

This book is about conducting ethnographic research in institutional sites of writing, such as writing programs, classrooms, curricular initiatives, and other areas of higher education. Informed by the lifelong work of Dorothy E. Smith, a Canadian sociologist, chapters explore, adapt, and expand "institutional ethnography" (IE) for writing studies researchers. Smith's career work recognized the highly personal, situated, and embodied nature of knowing and challenged traditional models of social science research. Positivist paradigms and universalist

DOI: 10.7330/9781607328674.c000b

models of empirical research in the social sciences, Smith (2005, 9) argued, frequently oversimplified and reified the material conditions of sites of study, objectifying research subjects. Instead, the model of ethnography Smith developed drew upon principles of feminist cultural materialism to focus the researcher's eye on the unique personal experiences and coordinated practices of individuals, as these revealed recurrent patterns of social organization. Smith, in short, "studied up"—a term popularized by Laura Nader (1972) in the early 1970s—to reveal elements of everyday experience that were often otherwise occluded, elided, or erased by qualitative models that sought to study predetermined aspects of culture and community. Smith (2006, 5) calls this the process of "looking up from where you are" a means of uncovering the knowing, doing, and being of active individuals who negotiate their everyday contexts in highly personal ways.

Ethnography itself is a well-known methodology in the field of writing studies. Defined by Linda Brodkey (1987b, 25) as "the study of lived experience," by Janice M. Lauer and J. William Asher (1988, 39) as a "kind of descriptive research [that] examines entire environments, looking at subjects in context," and by Clifford Geertz (1998) as simply "deep hanging out," ethnography offers an adaptable and reflexive means by which to explore the complex and highly networked terrain of interest to writing studies researchers, exposing, as Brodkey (1987a, 26) contends, "how, in the course of fabricating their lives, individuals also weave into their material cultures." Ethnography has largely been a go-to for researchers in writing studies because it offers a sense of richness and specificity that other forms of research may not, a "holistic view of the behaviors, beliefs, rituals, and interactions" central to those involved in sites of writing, as Elizabeth Chiseri-Strater (2012, 201) has argued.

While traditional ethnographers in writing studies are often interested in what is happening in sites of writing—what students or faculty are doing, for example—the IE project sets out to uncover *how things come to happen*, noting that "people participate in social relations, often unknowingly, as they act competently and knowledgeably to concert and coordinate their own actions with professional standards" (Campbell and Gregor 2002, 31). The methodology—or theoretical framework—of IE often focuses on the shape of people's "work," a concept defined generously (Griffith and Smith 2014). In IE, "work" denotes a series of coordinated practices within a local setting into which an individual routinely puts time and energy. It is through our work that institutions *coordinate the experiences and practices of individuals*, particularly in highly prescribed sites, such as "corporations, government bureaucracies, academic and professional discourses, [and] mass media," social complexes that have an inordinate power over the ways people go about their everyday lives (Smith 2005, 10). IE holds that individual experience, ideals of practice, local materialities, and institutional discourse are mutually constitutive; what individuals do is always rule-governed and textually mediated. Using IE to study the "work" that people carry out allows writing studies researchers to reveal the deep and often hidden investments and experiences of those people, making visible the values, practices, beliefs, and belongings that circulate below more visible or dominant discourses. The researcher might then uncover opportunities for recognition, conversation, or intervention.

A number of distinctive analytic moves are foundational to IE, but two are absolutely central to understanding the larger framework IE offers ethnographers: "standpoint" and "ruling relations." With both terms, Smith asks us to think about the socially organized and specifically regulated situation of individuals within institutions, a move that collapses distinctions between broader discursive forces (such as professional and institutional discourse) and the ways we carry out our work. Individuals are unique and knowing but also act from places of shared identity, professional alignment, and investment—their "standpoint." "Ruling relations" are "that extraordinary yet ordinary complex of relations . . . that connect us across space and time and organize our everyday lives" (Smith 2005, 8). Institutional ethnographers seek to trace the empirical bridges that connect these two points of understanding, noting that there is always a relationship between the "micro" and the "macro" elements of the sites they study (DeVault 2008, 4). The goal is to reveal how our lives take shape as a process of negotiation of social relations. As such, the IE framework shifts the ethnographer's eye away from reified or static understandings of the people, events, or sites studied. The methodology asks us instead to investigate how the individuals within a location co-create the dynamics and processes under investigation.

Writing studies researchers have long recognized that writing instruction is mediated through highly institutional, bureaucratized structures, but we have few specifically designed research tools to help us uncover the rich actualities of these sites that we have theorized so exactly. As writing studies researchers begin to account for the complex interconnections between the material conditions of our sites and how people do what they do, we begin to recognize how writing, writing pedagogy, and our multifaceted work in sites of writing are coordinated by particular institutional factors. These practices do not, indeed cannot, exist independent of local contexts and the unique individuals who bring them into being; they are always produced within situated contexts by actual people who are negotiating any number of professional, institutional, and highly individual ideals toward specific ends. IE offers researchers in writing studies a series of tools to begin to trace, unpack, and make visible the types of negotiation and coordination that are this process of co-constitution. We are better enabled then to understand how writing, writers, and writing instruction are shaped by the material conditions—labor, work, space, place, resources, and material aspects of culture—that surround, inform, and generate them. With tools like IE, we are able to generate rich research-driven stories that help us to talk back to these forces and their constraints. We benefit from the resulting opportunities to intervene in local contexts and reclaim our understanding of ourselves and our work on our own terms.

Reframing more traditional forms of ethnography through IE is a crucial move for writing studies research in the twenty-first century, an age marked by the rise of neoliberalism and increased austerity measures, as Nancy Welch and Tony Scott (2016), among others, have argued. In light of federal and state funding restrictions for public institutions (in accord with reduced support for the public sphere more generally), we've experienced a number of challenges to our ideals, our core pedagogies, and our notions of our expertise and value. These challenges are insistently reshaping our work in writing studies as they intractably remake the broader contexts of higher education.

Moreover, regularizing some aspects of ethnography (as *method*) using importable, scalable frameworks is crucial for revitalizing ongoing conversations about the particularities of ethnography in writing studies. Conducting ethnography (even critical ethnography) in and of itself does not necessarily set up a researcher to attend to the constructedness of institutional life or the actualities of our work, factors that must be considered to make effective research-driven changes to practice and policy or to effect program-wide improvement. IE poses the ongoing critical work of ethnography as a continuation of our theoretical, rhetorical, historical, and other discursive investments; but IE also grounds these critiques in the actualities uncovered by ethnographic practice. What is more, IE's attention to the rhetorical and material constitution of the institution and its adaptable heuristics offers an approach to ethnography that regularizes researchers' attentions to institutionally suppressed or standardized experiences so we can fully understand the work we carry out in institutional settings.

The focus on *our work* is key for understanding what IE offers that other methodologies do not. The material and the institutional have been concerns for writing studies for some time, and any number of ethnographic, empirical, and rhetorical methods may be and have been used to study the broader material relations of interest to our field (see, for instance, Welch and Scott 2016; Brandt 2014, Scott 2009; Sheridan 2012; Bishop 1999, among others). More narrow calls for studying and revising policy regarding writing program labor, labor relations, and the terms of our work (particularly in composition) have been central to ongoing conversations in writing studies as well (for example, Cox et al. 2016; Horner 2000, 2016).

However, as generative as these critical interventions are, we have lacked for methodologies that enable us to understand the situated actualities of our work within institutional contexts. The field has often been preoccupied with narratives of program design, curriculum development, and management—discourses that tend to standardize, generalize, and even erase the identities, expertise, and labor contributed by diverse participants. Scholarship in the field needs tools to help us deliberately compensate for that erasure. IE offers a comprehensive and situated means to uncover all the highly specific and individualized ways in which work actually takes shape within institutional settings. Research conclusions, program review, curricular and policy development (and subsequent recommendations), and other research-driven initiatives based on IE methodologies, I argue, are likely to be based on a more comprehensive understanding of how work proceeds in institutions and thus more likely to enable insights that initiate productive and lasting changes.

With its comprehensive framework for understanding how our work is institutionally generated and coordinated with the work of others, IE offers a working vocabulary and ready set of heuristics for new and practiced writing studies researchers interested in understanding the particularities of our everyday lives. This is a crucial step forward for our study of the impact of the labor conditions of the field and the relationships between pedagogy and material conditions and for further generating research-driven understandings of how our work with writers and writing instructors and in sites of writing may claim value, legitimacy, and support in the broader contexts of higher education.

ETHNOGRAPHY AS DEEP THEORY: WRITING AND MATERIAL RELATIONS IN THE NEOLIBERAL INSTITUTION

> *Much in the world of literacy, language, literature, and writing instruction has changed in the last decade. External entities have sought to shape our curricula, pedagogies, and teaching*

> *conditions and to promote their own agendas on assessment and professional development. Political and economic forces shape schools and public views of education. How we read, write, and learn continues to be transformed by technological and social forces. Against this complex backdrop stand our students, each with crucial needs and aspirations. NCTE remains committed to serving all students by drawing on all that we know about literacy, learning, and teaching.*
>
> —"An Update on National Council of Teachers of English Initiatives," members' email, March 15, 2016

> *One of the most important aspects of research methods and methodologies in rhetoric, composition and literacy scholarship has been the concerted effort to analyze and assess how writing, rhetoric, and literacy practices have been shaped by material constraints and realities.*
>
> —Eileen Schell, "Materialist Feminism and Composition Studies: The Practice of Critique and Activism in an Age of Globalization"

Institutional ethnography enters a field already attuned to many of the core questions, research practices, and epistemological challenges central to work with ethnography. Theresa Lillis (2008, 355) argues that the field's discussions of ethnography have typically been organized around two concerns: ethnography as *method* and ethnography as *methodology*. Unfortunately, Lillis also notes that these conversations have frequently explored writing in separation from the rich contexts that surround, shape, and produce it as a social practice, resulting in over-determined and operationalized understandings of writing, writers, and sites of writing in our research narratives. She poses instead that we re-conceive of ethnography as a form of "deep theorizing," that is, as a "fully fledged methodology and as a specific epistemology and ontology" (Lillis 2008, 355). That is, ethnography not only seeks to understand people, what they do, how they do it, and how their practices take shape, but in effect it theoretically constructs each of these interests as interdependent or relational. None of these points of ethnographic focus can exist in separation from the others.

Lillis's argument that ethnography can be understood as a form of "deep theorizing" offers an excellent starting point for this introduction's exploration of IE in today's neoliberal institution. But before we begin this exploration, we must first unpack a few more key terms and epistemological moves that are central to our ongoing conversation in writing studies about research and how we design and carry out projects. What, for instance, does it mean to distinguish ethnography *as method* from ethnography *as methodology*? Writing studies scholarship provides answers for us to build on:

> **Method:** Rebecca Rickly (2008, 261) defines method as the "variety of techniques for gathering data, such as participant observation, interviews, surveys, and so forth," focusing on how particular techniques of data collection provide more or less effective understandings of doing and knowing around our research interests.
>
> **Methodology:** This term has been defined as both "the underlying theory and analysis of how research does or should proceed" (Kirsch and Sullivan 1992, 2) and the means by which researchers "explore and track the dynamic and complex situated meanings and practices that are constituted in and by academic writing" (Lillis 2008, 355). In this vein of thinking, ethnography offers a "theoretically driven" approach to the design of research projects; as Beverly Moss (1992, 157) explains, "The theoretical perspectives that ethnographers adopt influence research questions, tools, and techniques of data collection and analysis, and the conceptual framework of the study itself." Similarly, Stephen Gilbert Brown and Sidney I. Dobrin (2004, 1) have argued that ethnography offers a "dialectical engagement between theory and practice," which grounds the field's central theories, pedagogies, and professional ideals in actualities that play out for real people.

As a method—the means by which we collect data—ethnography offers a standard set of practices: observations, interviews, surveys, textual analysis, and so on. As methodology, ethnography is commonly noted to be highly attuned to the social contexts of writing—a commonplace that aligns ethnographic practice with conceptions of writing currently active in the field.

This attunement to the situated nature of practices (such as writing) explains the continuing popularity of ethnographic research for writing studies researchers.[1] Scholars in the field have long put forward a vision of writing as "situated" (Smit 2004), a "social and rhetorical activity" (Adler-Kassner and Wardle 2015; Kent 1999), and dynamically responsive to the communities that generate, rely on, and engage with it (Berkenkotter and Huckin 2016; Swales 1990). We can see analogous sensibilities at work in Mary P. Sheridan's (2012, 73) description of the opportunities afforded the ethnographer: "Ethnography is highly responsive to the situation at hand, applying particular methods to specific issues or problems. Yet, what is distinctive about ethnography is its orientation to understanding the rich visible and seemingly invisible networks influencing the participants in the study. Through long time research, ethnography highlights the impact of these networks; in the process, ethnography examines perspectives that are often misunderstood, under developed, or occluded in popular understandings of an issue, thereby informing policies and practices that both affect the participants and inform the much-larger networks and structures in which these participants are located."

The field's long-term concerns for inclusion, social justice, and reflexivity align as well with other elements of research practice typically associated with ethnography, such as "collaboration [with research participants], the writing of multi-vocal texts, and the use of self-reflection on the part of the researcher" (Stinnett 2012, 130). Indeed, in one of the first texts to engage research methodologies and designs in composition, *Composition Research: Empirical Designs,* Lauer and Asher (1988, 45) argued that ethnography's concern for the social nature of writing not only produces a "rich account of the complexity of writing behavior" but does so with "a complexity that controlled experiments generally cannot capture." Lillis (2008, 354) further notes that the interest ethnographers display for social context arises out of "a deep pedagogic concern, as teachers around the world grapple with complex communication situations, often in the face of impoverished public discourses on language and literacy, as well as a growing awareness of the geopolitics governing writing for academic publication."

Even so, challenges to the epistemological and ontological centers of ethnography as a means by which to study writing are not difficult to find. Stephen M. North (1987, 278) takes the research method to task for its idiosyncratic, highly subjective, and insular results. Ethnography is of little use for developing authoritative study of a site, North concludes. Continuing this tradition of critique, Michael Kleine (1990) argues that writing studies ethnographers often fail to take a critical enough stance in their research narratives, overlooking pivotal relationships between the knower and what can be known—an oversight that casts suspicion on the empirical nature of the findings of ethnographic undertakings. Similarly, Carl G. Herndl (1991, 320) argues that it is the "imaginative power" or "persuasiveness" of the ethnographer's "narrative structures" (or "textual strategies") that makes ethnography a powerful form of sharing and understanding experience, but this recognition raises questions about the veracity and empirical nature of ethnography as a form of research.

In response to these critiques, ethnographers have adapted and evolved their stances, according to Brown and Dobrin (2004, 1–2), "discovering new sites for praxis, occupying new theoretical topoi, developing new signifying practices, articulating a new ethnographic subject, redefining [ethnography's] goals, reinventing its methodologies, and revising its assumptions in what constitutes a radical ontological and epistemological transformation." These arguments suggest that ethnography is keenly attuned to helping researchers uncover aspects of writing and sites of writing that other methodologies might not. These conversations also gesture to the importance of situating our chosen methods and methodologies firmly in the field of writing studies, offering models of research that are positioned within areas of our research interest but that methodologically extend and deepen our understandings of research practice as a local and grounded endeavor.

Cindy Johanek (2000, 33) notes the limits of generalized conversations about methods and methodologies, which lack "full analyses of research contexts." Johanek (2000, 35–36) argues that conceptualizing "research methods as merely methods and procedures devoid of context" tends to render them "difficult to grasp" and "meaningless without some grounding of purpose." Lillis (2008, 380) argues similarly, hinging her reconceptualization of ethnographic methodology as deep theorizing in the simultaneous recognition that *writing mediates geocultural difference*. Without writing, in other words, we cannot coordinate what people do and how they do it across time and space; the process of deep theorizing recognizes the generative and coordinating nature of *all* writing—"even as seemingly simple a text as a shopping list," as Charles Bazerman (1988, 8) would argue—which simultaneously engages material, historical, and cultural aspects of our social systems.

Twenty-first-century ethnographers, such as Elizabeth A. Campbell (2011, 10), contend that work with ethnography aligns well with efforts to study writing as "*constitutive*." Citing Peter Vandenburg, Sue Hum, and Jennifer Clary-Lemon, Campbell (2011, 10) argues that ethnography recognizes writing as "inextricably interrelated with the creation, organization, and continuing development of contemporary Western society, as well as the formation and evolution of individual identity." "To understand writing," Bazerman and Paul Prior (2003, 2) argue in parallel (though their focus tends toward linguistic analysis of writing, such as Critical Discourse Analysis), "we need to explore the practices that people engage in to produce texts as well as the ways that writing practices gain their meanings and function as dynamic elements of specific cultural settings."

Each of these researchers is arguing that we must acknowledge the ways our methods and methodologies produce the very grounds on which we claim understanding as researchers. More plainly, as Rickly

(2012, 262) notes, "Sociologist John Law maintains that 'methods, their rules, and even more method's practices, not only describe but also help to produce the reality that they understand.'" It follows, then, that to understand the nature of writing in institutional locations, we need an appropriately theoretical architecture for our research practice. IE is ideally suited to support this type of nuanced, emic, and holistic approach to institutionally situated writing research.

IE's approach collapses distinctions among writing, writing instruction, and the institution, framing writing as a discursive technology that enables people to negotiate, organize, and understand their institutional environments. Through its focus on the individuals carrying out the work of the institution, the IE framework enables us to answer current calls in the field to uncover how what we do in our classrooms and our programs and as writers or writing instructors is coordinated by the ideological and political discourses that imbue our lives and our work with meaning. IE enables us to systematically study the hierarchical systems of labor, professional systems of value, and notions of expertise and prestige that structure the realm of higher education, the field itself, and our local actualities as these are manifest in, around, and through writing.

Writing studies is a field intricately bound up with institutions. The institution of higher education provides an intellectual and physical location that supports, sanctions, regulates, and lends value to our work and interests. Writing and writing instruction themselves are institutional constructs, as Susan Miller (1993), David R. Russell (1991), Ellen Cushman (1999), and Ryan Skinnell (2016), among others, have argued. The literature of writing program administration, writing center studies, assessment, placement, and remediation have frequently given light to the intricate institutional negotiations that are undertaken by professionals who carry out these types of work (see, for instance, M. Harris 2002; Anson and Brown 1999; Bazerman and Russell 2002; Soliday 2002 as a small sample of authors who have treated institutional dynamics in their projects). This long recognition of the institution—as the site of our work and our field's professional grounding—has led to complex understandings of these locations in some of our research conversations. IE challenges us to push these visions toward further holistic complexity.

Descriptions of the institution, such as Elizabeth Ervin's (1996, 124), have noted the "complex relationships between discursive and material constructs" at the center of these social entities, contending that the field's institutionality acts as "what Mike Rose has called 'a political-semantic web that restricts the way we think about the place of writing in the academy.'"[2] Others, such as James E. Porter and colleagues (2000, 613), have posed institutions as "rhetorically constructed human designs" and suggested that members of the field position themselves within institutional settings through "reflection, resistance, revision, and productive action" to determine the most productive locations and strategies for change. Materialist theory, analysis, and critique has likewise directed scholarly attentions in writing studies to "a variety of material social relations" such as "work/life [and] institutional life," as these overlap with more persistent concerns for embodiment, difference, the materiality of texts, space, and actualities of experience (Schell 2012, 123). Meanwhile, recent scholarship on writing and place has also invoked the institution, as it has called writing studies researchers "to scrutinize how the locations of our work matter" and held that all locations are "formed by discursive options and by social and economic and political negotiations" (Shepley 2016, 3). These arguments readily align our work in writing studies with the materialist principles of IE.

IE further aligns ethnographic research with efforts to understand sites of writing more holistically. Conversations about the institutional organization of writing have at times reflected an inherently ecological perspective (calling up Marilyn Cooper's [1986, 364] "ecology of writing"). Mary Jo Reiff and colleagues (2015, 3), for example, argue that much of the scholarship of writing studies "envision[s] writing as bound up in, influenced by, and relational to spaces, places, locations, environments, and the interconnections among the entities they contain." Deborah Brandt and Tony Scott have similarly situated their understandings of the dynamic complexities of institutional contexts, posing the "economies of literacy" (Brandt 1998) and the "political economies of composition" (Scott 2009), respectively. With these moves, Brandt and Scott acknowledge that sites of writing are both responsive to and implicated in broader socio-political structures. Brandt, for instance, describes literate activity as a "resource" that is mediated by a series of powerful individuals, organizations, and institutions. Literacies engage students and their "sponsors" in "ceaseless processes of positioning and repositioning, seizing and relinquishing control over meanings and materials of literacy as part of their participation in economic and political competition. In the give-and-take of the struggles, forms of literacy and literacy learning take shape" (Brandt 1998, 173).

When we speak of an economy of literacy, we make visible the ways individuals, resources, and discourses, according to Brandt (1998, 178), "organize and administer stratified systems of opportunity and access."

Likewise, for Scott (2009, 16), recognizing that writing courses and the work of writing studies are situated within a "political economy" presumes "a dynamic and integrated relationship between individuals and their socio-political contexts." Like Lillis's work, Scott's project collapses the distinctions between broader socio-political structures (the macro) and the personal or local (the micro), illustrating that macro and micro processes of social organization act as "feedback loops." In the political economy, larger socio-political forces influence everyday practices, decisions, and judgments of real people. People, in turn, enact the policies, systems, and structures that perpetuate the social order. As Scott (2009, 18) writes, "Writing education isn't just shaped by political economic factors, it also produces the political economic."

Yet even with this attention to the dynamic social complexities of our institutional economies, we have far more work to do to understand the nature of our institutional lives and to study writing as institutionally constitutive. Despite the field's abiding concerns for how our programs produce notions of writing, pedagogy, and labor, *much of our field's discourse elides concern for what people are actually doing, how they are doing it, and how they are enabled to do it.* Herein lies the rub for much of the writing research that circulates in the field today. Some of our work remains notable for its focus on people and their experiences, sensibilities, and activities. However, a closer look at how we have theorized the institution (in the examples above, for instance) or an analysis of how we discuss the materialities of our institutional lives demonstrates far more attention to broad rhetorical patterns in the field, the university, and higher education *than to the ways individual people actually negotiate those discourses in an everyday sense.* As Richard H. Haswell (2005, 201) has argued, the field benefits from, but has not often made, "best effort inquiry into the actualities of a situation."

Institutional critique, for example, treats institutions and institutional structures as explicitly rhetorical, arguing that there is power in a project of re-seeing, as Porter and colleagues (2000, 633) have argued, "our disciplinary and institutional frames" as spaces of shifting opportunity and rhetorical intervention. In institutional critique, individuals *are present* as people doing the material work of the institution; however, beyond this, the project of institutional critique hovers above the actualities of on-the-ground experiences. Cultural material analyses, such as Bruce Horner's (2000) influential text *Terms of Work for Composition* and Marc Bousquet, Tony Scott, and Leo Parascondola's (2004) *Tenured Bosses and Disposable Teachers*, have similarly focused on the discursive work of key terms and the consequences of corporatist logics in higher education, revealing ideological investments and broad organizational strategies at the center of the field's labor relations. *Rarely have these critiques peered into the actualities of an individual's everyday work, however.* As such, they offer a limited picture of everyday experience and practice.

As a case in point, in the introduction to *Rewriting Composition: Terms of Exchange* (a text that revises and updates *Terms of Work for Composition*), Horner (2016, 1) embraces the project of cultural materialism, which "takes as a given the materiality of the 'conceptual,' as well as the 'conceptuality' of the seemingly purely material." With this move, Horner (2016, 1–2, original emphasis) doubles down on the theoretical nature of his project, posing it as an intervention into "conceptualizations *of* the conceptual as distinct from material." But, tellingly, as Horner (2016, 1) also notes that "readers who do not accept this argument will find the book frustrating," he acknowledges the constraints on his project. Critiques that stay at the level of the theoretical and the ideological absolutely help us to understand the generative schemas and reach of broader organizational patterns. Yet in telling half the story, these approaches are not necessarily as helpful as they might be to find points of intervention, buy-in, or investment.[3]

Despite this body of work, people and the actualities of their work and experiences are simply often elided from our field's ongoing discussions of our materialities. IE offers us an additional set of tools to complement and extend this ongoing effort to understand the material nature of writing, writing instruction, and our work in sites of writing. Continuing the project of understanding the everyday impact of twenty-first-century *materialities as actualities* is crucial to the realization of many of our field's projects. Ethnographers are prepared to step in to bridge this gap. Because ethnographers most often seek to uncover macro-social understandings of how people do what they do and the contexts that people must negotiate, ethnography, particularly forms like IE, allows ethnographers to theorize the intricate relationships among location, material cultures, and actual work.

In light of the increasing material constraints of our daily lives in the university as institution—where we remain in dire need of more explicit heuristics for studying the material realities that actively shape sites of writing and our lives as people who teach, study, and produce writing—this project responds to a here and now in writing studies that cannot be understated. Tony Scott (2009, 18) has argued similarly, noting that the field of writing studies has rarely attended to "writing education as concrete production." We may give lip service to contingency and exploitation, we may note how the field's patterns reflect managerial logics, we may discuss ideologies "as they play out in student texts and in writing classrooms" (Scott 2009, 19), but we seldom turn our attentions to the actualities of experience and practice that are the result of these political economies. Scott (2009, 19) writes: "Rather than rigorously seeking to understand how what we do is shaped by how we do it, the field's normal science continually sutures the split between disciplinary ambitions and projections and the material realities of writing education. It continually finds means of turning away from the contradictions that become apparent when the immediate and the material are juxtaposed with the structural and cultural."

Moreover, the professional situations of researchers—appointments as tenure-line faculty and writing program directors—frame the research interests, personas, and methods employed in our scholarly conversations, inevitably casting and presenting these concerns as administrative. The problem becomes that "systematic connections are rarely made between these factors and the character of literacy and learning as manifested in day-to-day classroom activity. In contrast, scholarly discussions of writing-pedagogy—method, purpose, and praxis in writing classrooms—tend to account for factors other than the institutional settings of writing education: textuality, rhetorical theory, ideology, technology, revision, gender, race, and so on. Though everyday institutional practices and the material terms of labor for teachers and students have a profound effect on the character of writing pedagogy, they don't often appear in research- or theory-driven discussions of postsecondary classroom pedagogy" (Scott 2009, 7). Scott's research has demonstrated the different types of stories that might emerge from work on how writing programs take shape within institutional economies (*qua* hierarchies).

IE is one more crucial response to these gaps. Because it turns the ethnographer's attention to actual people carrying out the work of the institution, IE speaks immediately to the concerns of writing researchers like Lillis, Scott, and others for how our work on writing, as writers, and in sites of writing is carried out in relation to the rich geocultural contexts and political economies/ecologies that generate that work. Through its theoretically grounded and systemic understanding of writing as constitutive, the framework enables us to answer current calls in the field to uncover how what we do is coordinated by the ideological and political discourses that imbue our lives and our work with meaning and value.

At this historical moment, IE responds to these increased calls in the field by offering a reexamination of the broad contexts of our work and how that work actually takes shape within our localities. The national landscape of higher education is being radically reshaped by the forces of neoliberal austerity (Welch and Scott 2016), a series of political and economic movements that have corporatized the governing structures of universities and threatened the material resources that support our work. Because ethnography is a research method that "examines perspectives that are often misunderstood, under developed, or occluded in popular understandings of an issue," it sheds light on "policies and practices that both affect the participants and inform the much-larger networks and structures in which these participants are located" (Sheridan 2012, 73). Ethnography, as such, remains among our most flexible tools for uncovering the actualities imposed on these networks and structures. IE, as this project argues, offers a means to continue these conversations with a sharper focus.

Research that systematically attends to how people must negotiate the landscapes created by austerity measures, material constraints, and local organizational efforts within their national and particular institutional contexts helps us understand our work in new ways. As institutional ethnographers observe, interview, and collaborate in work efforts with people—tracing the productive valence of texts in local settings and mapping the relationships that emerge—they offer a critical perspective on writing instruction as an institutional practice, investigate the ways we sustain programs and core philosophies that may find themselves under fire, and identify ways of intervening in larger systems that seek to reconstruct us in the image of the corporate university. Because IE foregrounds the standpoints of those who carry out their work in institutional venues, it serves to decentralize the focus of typical research activities in writing studies, bringing forward more and different perspectives and examining the positionalities that shape lesser recognized experiences (such as contingency, rank, HR designation, and union structures). The framework and analytic moves IE offers for understanding institutions and their impact on our work provide an opportunity for scholars to consider how our institutional affiliations and settings organize our most central ways of doing and knowing.

Putting institutional materialities at the center of our research on writing and writers does require us to be more deliberate in our approach to understanding sites as actual locations populated by real people. We gain enormously as researchers when we look into the relationships between the various pieces of the whole, seek to uncover the nature of that relationality, and draw tighter links between elements that might not, on the surface, appear to influence one another. We gain even more as a field when we develop methods that allow us to study the interconnections between seemingly discrete pieces of a dispersed social puzzle. IE allows us to bring our concerns for pedagogy, professional identity, disciplinary practice, labor, and other forms of materiality into conversation. The findings of the case studies shared in this project demonstrate exactly these dynamic interconnections among writing, the personal, the local, the everyday, and national discourse.

CHAPTER OVERVIEWS: THEORY AND PRACTICE

To undertake an IE project is to uncover the empirical connections between writing as individual practice and the conditions that make a site of study unique, "show[ing] how the organizational context invisibly shapes the practices of a site" (Townsend 1996, 179). More particularly, IE aids researchers interested in uncovering what local practices constitute the institution, how discourse may be understood to compel and shape those practices, and how norms of practice speak to, for, and over individuals. IE's focus on the day-to-day work life of individuals, as well as its emphasis on describing how individuals choose to interact with and within their institutions, provides a mechanism for naming, and thereby gaining insight into, the actualities of our academic work lives.

The following chapters explore the methodological (*qua* theoretical) and practical considerations of work with IE for understanding writing, demonstrating how I have used this methodology as a form of inquiry into the relationships between institutional locations and the writing-related practices that constitute them. The findings of each case study demonstrate the ways conceptions of writing (ruling relations) constitute the space studied and how people then use writing and a variety of related professional practices and identities (standpoint) to negotiate the landscapes they are situated within. As they do so, these case studies challenge the typical conceptualizations of pedagogy, labor, professional position, and the structure of programs currently active in the field, uncovering the situated relationality of these sites and the generative nature of institutional ways of doing, knowing, and being.

Because IE is at once a theory of institutional organization, a set of analytic moves that allow for a distinctive approach to analyzing and understanding a site and the people who carry out their work within that site, and a practical tool that aids writing researchers interested in how writing constitutes our work, chapter 1 has two goals. I begin with an exploration of the ways IE helps us to reframe our understandings of institutions as sites of writing (experience and practice), laying out the analytic moves IE offers for the study of how people do what they do in sites of writing as a means to negotiate their institutional standpoints.

The key analytic moves detailed in this chapter include ruling relations, standpoint, social coordination, problematic, work and work processes, and institutional circuits. This chapter draws on the corpus of work that has developed in sociology to then frame the possibilities of critical inquiries with IE for writing studies.

The remaining chapters offer different case studies that demonstrate IE in action in writing studies contexts—describing the theoretical framework that informed each study and the ways my own research practices took shape within complex institutional contexts. These chapters enact a praxis-driven exploration of the key terms in action, deepening and extending the theoretical model described in chapter 1. These chapters also uncover the highly relational nature of the terms, practices, and concerns that constitute our work in writing studies. My work with IE examines our professional conceptions of these terms, re-seeing the organizational work of these terms as a process of generalization that often erases and conceals more than it reveals.

Chapter 2 explicitly outlines the moves central to conducting a study with IE (from problematic to final analysis) and shares the findings of a study about how writing assignments took shape in a curricular initiative involving linked courses. This curricular initiative, referred to in this chapter as the "linked gateway," connected a large lecture (about the critical, historical, and theoretical frameworks for the study of literature) with a series of smaller writing courses that drew their content from the large lecture. Tracing the collaborative development of shared writing assignments in this hierarchical but collaborative setting, I argue, opens for deeper understanding how material actualities (such as patterns of labor, disciplinary identity, and ideals of writing instruction) coordinate the work of the sites we often study. This chapter is helpful to those who want to see IE in action, as I apply the central terms of the framework and explain how the key analytic moves of IE helped me uncover aspects of the site, particularly how the material relations of the site shaped conceptions of writing and subsequently the work of writing instruction. The findings of this study demonstrate that whereas members of the field have often posed pedagogy as a generalized conceptual tool or theory, pedagogy is instead a *highly individualized and material process* that invents and reinvents itself within situated, local, and material contexts as it organizes the particularities of work. The experiences and practices uncovered in this linked-course initiative allow us to reflect upon how the material contexts of our work in a local sense resist, refuse, and remake generalized ideals of pedagogy, as those ideals are driven by the field and its professional organizations.

Chapter 3 offers findings from a collaborative, cross-institutional study about the differences of experience and work for staff and faculty writing center professionals. Posing the HR distinction and annual review processes of writing center professionals as "boss texts" that govern the work actualities of people in hierarchical employment situations, this case study traces how these boss texts organize the labor of writing center professionals quite differently. With so much of the work in writing studies carried out by individuals, such as adjunct instructors and term faculty, who are increasingly articulated to universities and programs in tenuous and impermanent ways, this project demonstrates that an analysis of employment practices can inform writing researchers about the disjunctions and experiences that underwrite the day-to-day operations of writing programs, writing centers, and other significant sites of writing. This study demonstrates the power of IE for uncovering the disjunctions and erasures of experience that inform local practice. Our professional and personal discourses may gloss the very conditions that have produced the work of our programs—but in coming to closely analyze those missing elements of the stories we may tell, we see a fuller frame for understanding and mobilization.

Chapter 4 shares the results of a three-year study on the circulation of *information literacy* as a key term in a writing program for first-year students. In this chapter I argue that material actualities shaped classroom practice around *information literacy* instruction in ways that belied the recommendations of national statements and standards. Tracing the use of "information literacy" as it proliferated through sites of instruction, teaching conversations, and other moments on campus revealed the deeper values and investments active in the program and on campus. Findings reveal that instructors deployed the term as a means to negotiate both the landscape of the program and stakeholder expectations but did so in ways that enacted personal value systems, revealing highly individual understandings of the role of first-year writing in the preparation of student writers as researchers. Moreover, instructors and library faculty took up the term differently to manage the material conditions that influenced their everyday relations on campus. In this study, work with IE again reveals the ways the ideals of our work bump up against the coordinated nature of that work within local contexts.

These case studies argue explicitly for methodologies that allow writing studies researchers to uncover the local actualities of our work and to more effectively study the construction of our work and labor. With IE and similar research frameworks, we might better understand the impact conversations in the field have on what actually happens in our classrooms, programs, and cross-campus relations. As a field, we have become increasingly savvy about how the methods we choose shape the stories we are enabled to tell. Yet too often our research continues to generalize, and therefore over-determine, understandings of key terms and pedagogical concerns, turning away from opportunities to interrogate the grounds on which we make our most cherished arguments, identify and circumscribe research efforts, and continue ongoing research-driven conversations. I hope these case studies compel other ethnographers and researchers to ask: What other stories most need telling to internal and external audiences, and how might we continue to extend and deepen our thinking as writing researchers interested in institutional conditions? We have only just begun to uncover the ways our everyday actualities shape our work as writers, writing faculty, writing program administrators, and professionals in writing studies. As other researchers carry these questions forward, I look forward to the answers we will uncover.

1

INSTITUTIONAL ETHNOGRAPHY

A Theory of Practice for Writing Studies Researchers

> *Locating* the actual *as a distinct terrain of inquiry is one of the first challenges [of institutional ethnography]. We can hint at it by saying that underlying anyone's everyday life experience something invisible is happening to generate a particular set of circumstances. It is that "something" that is of research interest. People's lives happen in real time and in real locations to real people. Institutional ethnographers explore the actual world in which things happen, in which people live, work, love, laugh, and cry.*
>
> —Marie Campbell and Frances Gregor, *Mapping Social Relations: A Primer in Doing Institutional Ethnography* (original emphasis)

Conceptions of writing are closely imbricated with the actualities of our work as writing instructors, writing researchers, and people who work within the rich contexts of writing programs (Ohman 1976; Crowley 1998; Miller 1993; Horner 2000). Conceptions of writing constitute, organize, and shape the experiences and practices at the center of our work. Likewise, the organizational patterns of our work, the structures of our everyday lives, inevitably shape how we conceptualize writing. How, then, do we study these mutually constitutive relationships? In other words, how do we study how writing and writing instruction happen?

This chapter lays out and adapts the sociological framework of IE for the study of work in institutional sites of writing: classrooms, writing programs, writing centers, vertical writing curricula, campus cultures of writing, assessment initiatives, and other local and national sites where writing is the generative fulcrum that organizes institutional contexts. IE is "a method of inquiry designed to discover how our everyday lives and worlds are embedded in and organized by relations that transcend them, relations coordinating what we do with what others are doing elsewhere and elsewhen" (Griffith and Smith 2014, 10). The general goal of IE is to uncover *how things happen*—bringing

DOI: 10.7330/9781607328674.c001

to light the experiences and practices that constitute the institution, how discourse compels and shapes what people do, and how norms of practice speak to, for, or over individuals. IE focuses on the everyday work life of individuals, tracing work processes and textual mediations as these reveal the interplay among the individual, the material, and the ideological. The IE framework prompts us to ask how the experiences and practices of writing and its institutional structures (writing courses, writing instruction, and writing administration) are generated by the complex institutional contexts. How do we understand the material actualities of writing, writing instruction, and sites of writing? How does our work take shape?

As a "deep theory" (Lillis 2008), IE offers a process of inquiry for exploring how institutions take shape. IE as methodology poses the ongoing critical work of ethnography as a simultaneous process of theorizing our work within institutional contexts and as a means to understand the actualities of that work that live below the layers of our materialist discourse. In order to study writers, our work with writing instructors, our own work (as faculty and administrators), and sites of writing as a series of institutional relations—so that we surface the ways local institutional forces shape writing practices, writing instruction, and writing itself—ethnographers must be prepared with a flexible and adaptable set of heuristics, a critical working vocabulary, and a complex understanding of the ways these sites are co-constituted by knowing individuals who carry out their work in different settings. With its comprehensive framework for understanding how our work is institutionally generated and coordinated with the work of others, IE supports new and practiced writing studies researchers who would seek to understand the particularities of our everyday lives. The actualities we uncover deepen our ongoing efforts to understand the impact of the labor conditions of the field and the relationships between pedagogy and material conditions. The IE process of inquiry can help writing researchers study the complexities of institutional locations and the experiences and practices associated with writing, shifting the focus of study from what writers do "naturally" to account more fully for how writers, writing instructors, and writing administration negotiate their institutional contexts and material actualities.

Sections of this chapter define the key terms for work with IE in sites of writing: ruling relations, standpoint, social coordination, problematic, work and work processes, institutional discourse, and institutional circuits. Chapter 2 demonstrates how a project with IE is carried out, offering the case study of two linked gateway courses as the background.

HOW DO WE UNDERSTAND INSTITUTIONS?

Institutions are hierarchically ordered, rule-governed, and textually mediated workplaces, "organized around a distinctive function, such as education, health care, and so on" (Smith 2005, 225). Institutions are also complex rhetorical, social, and material entities, as scholars in writing studies have argued (see, for instance, Porter et al. 2000; Horner 2016; Schell 2003; the introduction to this volume). As ethnographers who study writing and the conditions that surround, shape, and produce writing, we want to enter sites with our eyes open to often hidden, erased, or elided experiences and practices that live below our preconceived notions of institutionally organized work.

Most of us tend to have a "generalized macro-level ideal" in mind when thinking about or discussing institutions and large formalized organizations (LaFrance and Nicolas 2013). That is, we share a collective understanding of these sites based on common preconceptions and experiences in and around them (Smith 2005, 160). The challenge for the institutional ethnographer is to recognize the dynamic and generative nature of the institution as a social entity. IE supports this move by conceptualizing individuals as unique and knowing while emphasizing how institutions function as "shape-shifters," social constellations that adapt to the distinctive needs and roles of the individuals who engage them. The "university," for example, looks quite different from individual to individual. As Melissa Nicolas and I explain, "A professor experiences 'university' very differently from the student who experiences 'university' very differently from her parents who, again, experience 'university' very differently from the trustees. And even an individual's micro-level account of 'university' changes over time: a first-year student has a different relationship with 'university' than a senior whose definition will change as she becomes an alumnae" (LaFrance and Nicolas 2012, 131).

Institutions of higher education, campus communities, writing programs, professional positions, and classrooms come into being in the moments in which people negotiate the everyday toward some highly individualized end. In noting the mutable nature of the institution, we are able to refocus our ethnographic eye on people as they negotiate their environments. We are able to challenge our own presumed or static understandings imposed by institutional or professional discourses. We are able to trace patterns of behavior that emerge over time and space as we compare, contrast, and make associations within and across sites, observing how people in similar situations do what they do.

To trace these mutually constitutive relationships, IE focuses the researcher on what people do in the everyday—the practices they engage in, the decisions they make about those practices, and how their negotiations of policy, procedure, hierarchies, and systems of value take on a particular shape. On the one hand, these everyday experiences and practices are a matter of choice, preference, and personal forms of identification; on the other hand, because institutions are material locations and social relations have material implications, these everyday doings are influenced by the common ways of doing, knowing, and being that are active social and professional norms in local settings. It is the "doing" of people who are situated in time and space that brings these tensions into visibility, making the institution itself legible for study (Smith 2001, 163). A focus on the doing of people and attention to how they do what they do within institutional contexts allows the institutional ethnographer to bring new insights to the study of writing as a material face of the institution.

Because IE sees institutions as hierarchically ordered, rule-governed, and textually mediated *workplaces* and as complex rhetorical, social, and material entities that shape what we do and how we do it, ethnographers who adapt the IE framework can systematically account for individual practices within the interconnected sites of programs, units, and institutions. IE is concerned with the specifics of difference, divergence, and disjunction within sites of writing; it brings to visibility what happens in local sites below the level of professional, managerial, pedagogical, and other free-floating discourses. The methodology offers us the opportunity to uncover and explore stories that are often otherwise erased by the field's preoccupation with generalized disciplinary and pedagogical ideals.

Consider the following three vignettes:

> A TA who has agreed to be a participant in my study of a linked gateway course for English majors is telling me about an assignment she is teaching in her section of the writing link. The professor who wrote the assignment prompt (a "commentary") is a senior scholar in the field she hopes to enter and is in charge of the lecture her writing course is linked to. But the TA tells me she has never heard of or written a "commentary" and so isn't sure how to answer the questions her students are asking about the assignment. "It's sort of like a summary, only there's more to it than that," she tells me as she recounts the prompt. "[The professor] says it isn't structured like an argument. It's more focused on plot and character—I think. My students keep asking me what I want them to do. I keep asking him what he wants me to do." [*Laughter.*]

* * *

> I am meeting with a representative of the HR office because there has been some confusion over the title of a position in the writing center I supervise. Is the employee's title "Assistant Director of the Writing Center" or "Writing Center Assistant"? Because the position is currently classified as "staff" and

has been assigned to a particular "pay band," the representative tells me that the person in the position must adhere to a regular eight-hour workday and work full-time during the breaks between semesters (when the center is closed and there is little daily "work"). The position must be focused on "front desk" duties—answering the phone and email, keeping the schedule of appointments, submitting tutor time cards, and doing other paperwork. The person in the position cannot be asked to tutor more than eight hours weekly, which includes covering shifts when tutors miss them. The individual in the position can volunteer to run workshops or work on resources for tutor training if they choose but cannot be tasked with this regularly.

As I listen to the representative, I am thinking about how I'd like to see the "Assistant Director" provide a professional model to our tutors—tutoring, leading tutor trainings, and also teaching first-year writing classes. I believe an "Assistant Director" should be working with me to develop and support a culture of writing that sustains the tutor development work beyond initial training and workshops. I want us to move away from thinking that the work of the center is about "correctness" or is "secretarial" in nature. The HR representative tells me that this move would entail a reclassification of the position, from staff to faculty, require the prior approval of the dean's office, and require that the position be held in an academic department, such as English. I begin to realize, then, that the structure of this position will largely be determined by a number of factors that may well be beyond my control.

* * *

In a "think-aloud protocol" recorded for me, an instructor verbalizes her thoughts as she composes a writing assignment involving library research for first-year writing students. About seven minutes into her recording, her voice takes on a slight note of frustration. She describes going to the library website to find resources for her students but feeling like what she wants her students to be doing doesn't match what the library seems to think they should be doing. Three times, she repeats the circular process of going to the campus library's website to look for resources or links that will be helpful to her students, not finding what she is looking for, then returning to her handout.

After typing and deleting a sentence that asks her students to go to the library website to look at resources themselves, she confides to the digital recorder:

> What I'm realizing about situated research practices is that . . . [*five-second pause . . . and heavy sigh*] . . . that if I'm researching a community there may be some things that are valuable on the library website. But a lot of what will be happening in this research process is that my students will be gathering general information about their communities and specific information about one community . . . and that will lead me outside of the typical realm of academic research.
>
> So I guess the question that comes up for me is, what is academic research? What is it not? I don't want my students to have to

> be doing the kind of work a graduate student or a person with a doctorate is doing. I don't think they have the resources to, and it will just make them hate life. So I keep coming around back to—how do I make this process manageable for them? And how do I make it accessible for them?

In the first vignette, a TA struggles to understand how to teach a writing assignment designed by someone else. The "commentary," a genre that is popular in some schools of literary analysis, is a form unfamiliar to this TA, who must coach her students through the form and grade their written responses to the prompt. The TA reveals her struggle with the guidance she is getting from the professor who designed the assignment. As she recounts her attempts to make sense of the assignment, she compares it to other genre forms she is familiar and comfortable with—but seems to suggest that these comparisons are not helping her understand the assignment as she would like. This vignette reveals the ways writing is negotiated into being between those employed as TAs in the linked courses and the ways the linked-course structure influences particular understandings of writing. Writing, as it is conceived of within the social networks of the linked gateway courses, takes shape in the interplay among the professor, the professor's writing prompt for undergraduates, and the conversations TAs carry forward to student writers who complete the assignment.

The second vignette reveals different visions of writing center work through conversations about the shape and focus of an employee's workday. The HR office has put forward a standardized set of expectations for the work of staff members within a particular "pay band" and seeks to shape the position's daily tasks to reflect those expectations. The investment of the HR office is in creating consistently fair expectations for all employment situations at the university and keeping the university in compliance with county, state, and federal employment regulations. These standardized ideals of work do not match my vision for the work of an "Assistant Director," as these ideals have been inspired by professional conversations within the writing center community. The ideals of writing center work that I espouse are closely imbricated with theories of writing that (1) are active in writing studies; (2) recognize the situated, flexible, and rhetorical nature of writing; and (3) conceive of work with student writers as a form of professional expertise. The divergent visions we have for the employee's title and daily duties demonstrate the difficulties inherent in situating the work of writing studies professionals within preexisting institutional structures. Across campus, elements of that work, such as a title and the scope of daily work practice, will look dramatically different to those involved in this discussion because of our distinctive professional investments in and institutionally situated perspectives on the nature of that work. We often think of titles and our work in generalized ways, without much attention to how these sites of our work actually take shape in the local contexts that inform and shape them.

In the third vignette, we see an instructor of a first-year writing course thinking through a question to which the field of writing studies has no fewer than dozens of different responses. From Ambrose N. Manning's query in 1961 about whether the "research paper" was "here to stay," to Ken Macrorie's 1988 proposal for *I-Search* that pitched "research" as a form of inquiry, to Joseph Bizup's (2008) call to teach research as a "rhetorical practice," to Elizabeth Wardle's (2009) critique of composition's reliance on "mutt genres" including the "research paper," to efforts by the Citation Project team to understand how students approach sources in their reading and writing (Howard, Serviss, and Rodrigue 2010; Jamieson and Howard 2011), there is little agreement in the field of writing studies about what constitutes "research" or how students best learn the basic conventions of "research." Even so, this instructor seems to be bumping up against her university library's established set of expectations for student writers. There is an interesting moment in the participant's response, which is the sort of significant "tell" an ethnographic researcher is always looking for: the participant pauses and sighs deeply, demonstrating an emotional pause. (She tells me later in an interview that she felt what she was doing didn't match *what she thought she was expected to do.*) What we see in this instructor's narrative is an example of an individual negotiating a variety of different expectations placed on her work teaching a writing class.

The foundational tenet of IE becomes clear in these three vignettes—in the doings represented here, we can begin to see how notions of writing and its institutional contexts are *co-created* in the "inter-individual" interplay among discursive structures, material actualities, and the work individuals carry out (Smith 2005). The conceptions of writing in each vignette are constructed through these "discursive pivot points" (DeVault 2008, 5) that take shape in the moments when knowing and active individuals engage in their work. These vignettes then reveal how institutional contexts contour the conceptions of writing they generate. As the individuals in each vignette interact with one another to engage in a series of practices related to writing, they are each negotiating individual understandings of the purpose, character, and value of their work. The experiences of these individuals and the multifaceted conceptions of writing that emerge in these interactions are shaped by any number of factors: how the local hierarchy informs the situation, the professional affiliations and identities of those involved, the adherence of those involved to norms of communication, interpretations of policy and procedure, popular versus scholarly conceptions of writing, and any number of other rather personal understandings of the role and stakes of the interaction. The institutional ethnographer can then track similar discursive pivot points and the constructions of writing that emerge in these interactions, revealing the impact of the material conditions within a setting. In tracing these generative moments, we uncover the materialist grounds on which writing takes it shape.

These vignettes reveal a crucial element of work with IE. Writing, writing pedagogy, and our multifaceted work in sites of writing are never entirely untouched by institutional factors. These practices do not, indeed cannot, exist independent of local contexts and the unique individuals who bring them into being. In fact, these central concerns for the field of writing studies are always produced within situated contexts by actual people who are negotiating any number of professional, institutional, and highly individual ideals toward specific ends. IE offers researchers in writing studies a series of tools and heuristics to begin to trace these processes of negotiation.

AN INSTITUTIONALLY SAVVY METHODOLOGY: THE HEURISTICS OF IE

> *Most often, we study horizontally, or down.*
> *Much more rarely do we study up.*
>
> —Wendy Bishop, *Ethnographic Writing Research: Writing It Down, Writing It Up, and Reading It*

> *Institutional ethnography begins by locating a standpoint in an institutional order that provides the guiding perspective from which that order will be explored. It begins with some issues, concerns, or problems that are real for people and that are situated in their relationships to an institutional order. These concerns are explicated by the researcher in talking with them and thus set that direction of inquiry.*
>
> —Dorothy Smith, *Institutional Ethnography: A Sociology for People*

The IE framework reveals that writing takes shape in a complex chemistry among individuals, social relations, and material conditions. The three vignettes above offer snapshots of the interplay among people, professional and institutional discourse, and the many policies, procedures, and material actualities that structure institutional contexts. When we begin to ask how things actually happen—how it is that writing, writing instruction, and our work in writing programs takes shape—we are poised to collect information about the processes individuals undertake as they negotiate the everyday contexts of their work lives. As IE uncovers the situated variability of experience and practice within institutions, it offers researchers in writing studies the opportunity to more effectively study how individuals mindfully negotiate the competing priorities and material conditions of their workdays and how the discourses of educational sites, writing instruction, writing programs, and writing itself bind individuals to particular workplace, educational, and cultural philosophies.

Writing is always a product of these webs of the social. Ideals of generalized practice may coordinate the actions individuals carry out, organizing their daily lives around key notions of the value of labor, access, and institutional mission. However, through individual experience and practice, as these require the negotiation of the social, institutional, and professional worlds, writing and sites of writing take shape. As we think more intentionally about how the roles, interests, needs, expectations, and desires of individuals in a site are mediated within and by institutional contexts, we can begin to uncover and examine the range of practices that constitute writing that live below institutional discourses. We may come to understand how our generalized conceptions (of writing, of writing pedagogy, of best practices in writing instruction, of writing program organization) actually play out on the ground for real people.

Like other forms of ethnography, IE draws on the sustained data-collection techniques typical in more traditional forms of ethnography: interviews, case studies, focus groups, textual analysis, discourse analysis, auto-ethnography, participant observation, think-aloud protocols, and archival research. In most traditional forms of ethnographic research, the ethnographer describes what people do. Since the late 1970s, a number of emergent forms of critical ethnography have become increasingly concerned with context, an understanding that people are situated within powerful and at times coercive social contexts. IE aligns with ethnographic projects concerned with context, noting that how people are positioned within a site will often dramatically impact not only what people do but how they do it. Smith (2006, 5) describes the analytic process of IE as a matter of "looking up from where you are" to study how personal experiences (and so, work practices) express a social order. Marjorie L. DeVault and Liza McCoy (2006, 20) describe the general process of IE research more generally, noting that the process entails "(a) identify[ing] an experience, (b) identify[ing] some of the institutional processes that are shaping that experience, and (c) investigat[ing] those processes in order to describe analytically how they operate as the grounds of experience." Institutional ethnographers may begin by reflecting on personal experiences within or around a site, or they may institute exploratory processes of surveying, interviewing, or observing individuals to get a sense of the "language, thinking, concepts, beliefs and ideologies" that constitute a site (Luken and Vaughan 2005, 1604).

The methodology gains its rigor and systematicity from a series of distinctive analytic moves that enable this process of "looking up" and drawing connections between the individual and the social realm that surrounds and shapes practice. As Marie Campbell and Frances Gregor (2002, 29) explain, "Analytically, there are two sites of interest [to the institutional ethnographer]—the local setting where life is lived and experienced by actual people and the extra-local that is outside the boundaries of one's everyday experience." When data-collection activities have resulted in a reliable body of data, the institutional ethnographer will begin to analyze how individuals speak of and engage in their daily practices, thinking about how participant responses and practices reveal the ongoing coordination of activity. Variations, disjunctions, disagreements, or absences may reveal themselves in the rationales enabled by this process of "looking up," as these complex moments tell a story about the ways personal experience and work practices have been reflexively contoured by the material and discursive conditions of the site (Campbell 2003, 4). The narrative an institutional ethnographer composes will explicate the confluence(s) of individual experience, work practice, and dominant discourses at each location, demonstrating "an empirical bridge between local and particular processes," as it brings to light the ways individuals actively negotiate the "social relations that order everyday existence" (Luken and Vaughan 2005, 1604).

There are seven core concepts that shape work, with IE providing a means of both theorizing our research interests and analyzing institutional relations: *ruling relations, standpoint, social coordination, problematic, work and work processes,* and *institutional circuits.* The remainder of this chapter summarizes and explores these concepts to provide readers with a general sense of IE's approach to research inquiry. Later chapters take up and apply these concepts through case studies designed following the principles of IE.

Ruling Relations

> *The point of following social relations is to see how people in one place are aligning their activities with relevances produced elsewhere.*
>
> —Marjorie L. DeVault, *People at Work*

Analogous to powerful social and workplace norms, "ruling relations" draw upon and influence institutional patterns, such as hierarchies, allocation of resources, and work processes. These relations coordinate and/or organize daily experiences and practices, influencing what people do and how they do it across space and time. Smith (2005, 8) writes that ruling relations are both "extraordinary yet ordinary," a constellation of social relations that coordinate the everyday experiences and practices of people in different settings, carrying out different work. Ruling relations, then, echo throughout the different layers of institutional and professional organizations—appearing in the broadest discourses of national and professional organizations—but also permeate the everyday rationales and often unspoken assumptions that order local processes and patterns of decision-making. Working conditions and daily routines bear traces of ideology, history, and social influence.

Yet it is important to recognize that, as Campbell and Gregor (2002, 31) expound, "Social relations are not done to people, nor do they just happen to people. Rather, people actively constitute social relations. People participate in social relations, often unknowingly, as they act competently and knowledgeably to concert and coordinate their own actions with professional standards or family expectations or organizational rules." As people act with purpose and knowledge, they act in concert with professional standards and the expectations of organizations, colleagues, and employers. Participating in these forms of social organization naturalizes the multitudes of practices that imbue a site, making them "just how it's done" and easily taken for granted. Ruling relations make themselves visible when we see over time and space how the work of one person (or a small group of people) bears similarities to the work of others in other programs, classrooms, or locations. When we see writing teachers or writing programs, for instance, share vocabulary, philosophies of writing, and similar sorts of assignments or when those we interview independently tell the same stories, reflect on the same moments, discuss the same issues, or offer a shared sense of purpose, ruling relations are coming into visibility.

It is in this term that we see Smith's most explicit nod to Marxist cultural materialism. While Smith tends to situate her work against more mainstream sociological theorists, such as Simmel, Durkheim, and

Giddens, there is a strong resonance in her discussion of social mechanisms with Gramscian notions of the relationship among the everyday, ideology, and hegemony (see, for instance, *Selections from the Prison Notebooks,* 1971). For Antonio Gramsci, the social order was maintained through a variety of coercive forces, but dominant ideologies tended to cast the social order as the inevitable outcome of the relations of production. Smith's arguments on ruling relations resonate as well with Stuart Hall's (1985, 113–14) argument that ideology "articulates individuals into cultural forms": "By the term 'articulation,' I mean a connection or link which . . . requires particular conditions of existence to appear at all, which has to be positively sustained by specific processes, which is not 'eternal' but has constantly to be renewed, which can under some circumstances be overthrown, leading to the old linkages being dissolved and new connections—re-articulations—being forged."

These powerful ideals and representations take shape around "forms of consciousness and organization that are objectified in the sense that they are constituted externally to particular people and places" (Smith 2005, 13). Ruling relations are most visible as they give shape to actualities of experience and practice.

When writing studies researchers adapt a heuristic such as ruling relations, they are seeking to understand the patterns of social organization, conditions of work, experience, and practice that give a sense of character or identity to a site and the work we carry out within that site. More particularly for a field or disciplinary community like writing studies, ruling relations show themselves in established disciplinary discourses and the professionalization of practice. The statements, standards, noteworthy publications, and ideals of "best practice" sanctioned by the leading membership organizations in the field, such as College Composition and Communication, the National Council of Writing Program Administrators, the International Writing Center Association, and the International Network of Writing across the Curriculum Programs (among others), often influence and organize what people do and how they do it within writing programs and classrooms.

Writing studies has a number of central professional statements that not only have made clear the values that are active in the field but are used programmatically by members of the field to structure the work of writing courses, writing programs, and the labor of writing teachers. The "WPA Outcomes Statement" (Harrington et al. 2001), "The Principles for the Postsecondary Teaching of Writing" (CCCC Executive Committee 1989), and "Evaluating the Intellectual Work of

Writing Program Administrators" (WPA Executive Committee 1996) have all played a significant role in clarifying what writing programs do, the conditions under which students and teachers might best do their work, and the ways the leadership of writing programs might be structured. Professional statements not only provide educators with a generalized sense of the ideals of practice and prevailing sensibilities within writing studies, but they are also useful to programs and departments in making crucial arguments about the value of the work faculty do in their classrooms and within campus communities, the working conditions necessary for success, and appropriate types of teaching practice to administrators and colleagues who may have different ideas about how writing courses should be organized, staffed, or situated in a curriculum.

In a more programmatic sense, these statements guide the adoption of key terms and certain pedagogical approaches in writing classrooms, impacting which textbooks might be chosen for writing classes and shaping the ways writing is instructed through assignments, classroom activities, and instructional interactions. As Smith (2005, 60) writes, "There is no concept that is not a relational term." As epistemological frameworks, these statements idealize aspects of student learning and create visions of professional identity and purpose. As professional standards, they endorse and sanction particular types of practice as they draw on the collective and dynamic vision writing studies professionals will then carry out with students and colleagues in local settings. Reading these documents as demonstrations of ruling relations helps us understand the ways members of the field collaboratively co-construct their visions of the field, its authority, and our work. Thinking about professional statements in terms of ruling relations helps us explore where the concepts and practices that are considered "best practices" may originate and how they may function in classrooms, in programs, and for particular individuals. They help us think more strategically about how best practices enter the sites we study. They help us think about who authorizes ideals of practice or who is positioned to pass particular practice on to others.

The scholarship of our field is yet another level of discourse that can be read as a complex of powerful ruling relations. The top journals in a field can be said to establish the centers of professional conversation and therefore disciplinary and sub-disciplinary identities central to scholarly work. National and regional conferences order themselves similarly around the core concepts that have generated the most interest in the field—think "writing transfer," "translingualism," "re-mixing," or "building community" to echo some recently popular writing studies conference themes. Anyone who has attended the annual Conference on College Composition and Communication can hear the echoes of these ruling discourses in the prevalence of particular terminologies, pedagogical stances, and philosophies that regularly appear on a program. It is through these central conversations that the field argues its investments and value systems, establishing a recognizable sensibility that will underwrite the community of practice at large.

Standpoint

> *Standpoint epistemologies have long counted among the most powerful challenges to the conventional view that true knowledge is value-free, disinterested, and situationally transcendent. Severing the traditional epistemological linkage between objectivity and neutrality, and measuring truth claims in terms of particular social locations and experiences, standpoint theories typically assert that scientific knowledge is inescapably position-bound, and hence both partial and partisan in character.*
>
> —Dick Pels, "Strange Standpoints, or How to Define the Situation for Situated Knowledge"

Where ruling relations enable institutional ethnographers to trace broad social patterns, "standpoint" helps the ethnographer to uncover the disjunctions, divergences, and distinctions experienced by individuals within those groups. In a general sense, standpoint refers to an individual's unique perspectives, attitudes, or position, recognizing that the way an individual must be in the world is often highly prescribed. Knowledge, experience, and our related personal situations are highly individualized but are also constantly shaped by historical, cultural, and social values and beliefs.

Feminist critical theorists of the 1970s and 1980s came to "standpoint theory" as a challenge to the notion of universal or purely "conceptual" knowledge. Dorothy Smith (1974, 8) was among the first of these feminist voices to critique the traditional empirical models of sociology, which excluded women's experiences and perspectives from "its methods, conceptual schemes, and theories."[1] Smith argues that a masculinist understanding of social relations—which privileged abstraction, objectivity, and a disembodied subject—dominated and therefore structured mainstream sociological thought. In Smith's (1974, 10) words, women and the concerns of women had been both "outside and subservient to this structure." The resulting universalist approaches to sociological study erased and marginalized difference of experience, being, and knowing—restricting what could be known, studied, and understood.

Expanding through the 1980s to include any group or individual that identified as marginalized,[2] standpoint theory helps researchers understand that, as Sandra Harding (2004, 3) writes, "the social order looks different from the perspective of [the] lives and [the] struggles [of those marginalized by the social order]." The conceptual frameworks that pose universals—as objective or pure *truths*—are also, as Dick Pels (2004, 273) writes, "position-bound, and hence both partial and partisan in character." Recognizing all knowledge as the product of a particular epistemological framework allows us to understand a richer range of experiences. For, as Donna Haraway (1988, 584) argues, "objectivity turns out to be about particular and specific embodiment, and definitely not about the false vision promising transcendence of all limits and responsibility. The moral is simple: only partial perspectives promise objective vision. This is an objective vision that initiates, rather than closes off, the problem of responsibility for the generativity of all visual practices."

This situated knowledge can be understood as a co-constructed web, emerging from individual experience and informed by processes of marginality, identity, and affiliation/belonging. This is not to imply that standpoints are static; the relationships between identity and material situations are often complex and always evolving in the moment. Further, an individual standpoint is not necessarily representative of a whole group of people. Through exploration of standpoint, the complexities and connections between individuals can be uncovered. That is, standpoint reveals that an individual's work is always coordinated within an institutional landscape.

In the IE framework, standpoint recognizes that we are implicated in social networks in ways that may not always be entirely clear. But when we think about the interplay among the material conditions of our work within particular settings, our social alliances or connections to different networks, and what discourses influence our everyday work practices, we can begin to see how particular locations materially situate us, accounting for the differences that are generated. As Smith (1974, 13) writes, "The actualities of our everyday world are already socially organized. Settings, equipment, 'environment,' schedules, occasions, etc., as well as the enterprises and routines of actors[,] are socially produced and concretely and symbolically organized prior to our practice." Because standpoint theory and the work of the institutional ethnographer is "post-positivist" in its approach, as DeVault and Glenda Gross (2012,

176) explain, the institutional ethnographer must "reject" the notion that social realities are neutral or just waiting in some pure form to be uncovered in their unadulterated forms: "Instead, we understand the social contexts of people's lives as historically situated and constituted through people's activities, and the research process itself as an integral aspect of the construction of knowledge about society . . . These are never matters solely related to collecting, analyzing, or presenting data, but instead are modes of thought and action that continually inform these mutually constitutive stages of the research process." As such, an individual's social alliances, experiences, and sensibilities play a defining role in how that individual negotiates everyday institutional settings and sites of writing (such as classrooms, programs, or departments).

An embrace of standpoint materially situates not just the participants in the research study but also the researcher in the narratives that are generated. The uniqueness of individual experience—both what the researcher already knows about a site from personal experience and what she has come to understand from her work interviewing and observing those she has set out to learn from—"provides the guiding perspective" for the research narrative that may be produced (Campbell 2003, 94). Janet Rankin and Marie Campbell (2009, n.p.) refer to "expert insiders" as a way of clarifying the term, a move useful for researchers in writing studies, acknowledging the ways writing expertise is itself a situational category, a product of socialization into a community of practice (or discourse community) as well as specialized literacies. The researcher takes on a materially mediated role with the site within this framework.

The embrace of standpoint for writing researchers has a number of important implications. We can move away from making claims that our research produces objective and easily replicable understandings. We might think in more savvy and nuanced ways about how our research offers more points of illumination, understandings of difference, and critically inflected representations as we map the experiences and practices of others in our classrooms and programs. For institutional ethnographers who study writing, standpoint also supports a focus on what we bring to a study: experience managing, researching, and teaching in writing classrooms and writing programs as professionals within a research-driven discipline. As members of the professional community of writing researchers ourselves, we have enormous personal and professional stakes in the effective negotiation of our own institutional terrains. As a field, we have already attended to a number of issues closely related to the concerns of the institutional ethnographer: marginality, diversity, and difference. As teachers, program leaders, and colleagues, we know firsthand how material and working conditions have ordered everyday relations to writing. With more attention to how our work is materially situated, we may also begin to explore the very different ways the individuals we work with conceptualize and experience writing, writing classrooms, and writing programs.

Social Coordination

Social relations "hook people" (Smith 2005, 40) into the established ways of doing, knowing, and being co-constituted by people who participate in an established social order. When our actions are "coordinated," we may find ourselves engaging in complex actions with others across time and space. To explain, Campbell and Gregor (2002, 29) offer the example of riding a campus bus: people wait for the bus at a bus stop. When the bus arrives, they line up to board, and as they board, each shows a card to the driver who allows them entry. People sit in empty seats and ride to their destination. "The actions of the bus driver are coordinated with those of the students who wait for, then board, the bus. Their actions are coordinated with his" (Campbell and Gregor 2002, 29–30). Even if people do not know each other well, they negotiate these interactions in a number of ways, responding to social cues, deferring to (or resisting) authority, engaging with texts, mimicking and learning from the actions of others, and following patterns of behavior.

Smith's arguments about social coordination forward the work of cultural materialists, as she notes the unfolding, renewable, and historical nature of social forms. Grounding the social science project of IE in Marx and Engels's critique of the German ideologists, Smith (2005, 65) argues that history and society do not exist independently of people's activities: "The social might be conceived as an on-going historical process in which people's doings are caught up [in] and responsive to what others are doing; what they are doing is responsive to and given by what has been going on; every next act, as it is concerted with those of others, picks up and projects forward into the future." And so, common forms of social organization grant practices legitimacy within institutions ("that's the way we've always done it"), discursively mobilizing individuals into everyday experience and practice in ways that are specifically sanctioned by prevailing notions of labor and value.

In a writing program or class, we might see social coordination as we start to investigate any number of common practices, from the formal and informal protocols people follow at copy machines, to where people sit or stand in a classroom, to the ways courses are designed to reflect a program's mission or outcomes, to more infrequent practices, such as annual employment reviews, submitting scholarly writing for publication, or attending a conference. Each of these everyday activities (and many, many others) carries forward complex social processes, which regulate and at times impose actualizations, generalizations, and differentiations. The social order lends value to particular modes of *doing, knowing, and being.* These visible forms of coordinated experience and practice are perpetually constructed and reconstructed through the active participation of individuals within the established organizational schemas of their everyday contexts.

Problematic

A "problematic" is not necessarily a "problem," such as the issue of low pay per course for contingent faculty. A problematic may begin with such a problem, but it then recognizes and accounts for the situated, complex, and interconnected relations among people, their experiences, and their practices related to that problem. So, for instance, while low status for contingent faculty may indeed trigger a study within an institutional site, the questions we start with as institutional ethnographers must focus on "set[ting] out a project of research and discovery" that is unique to the people and site under study (Smith 2005, 38). Situating ethnography within institutional settings as an *exploration of a problematic* (over a set of rote research questions) foregrounds the relational and material nature of institutional experience, a recognition that not all individuals will be oriented to a practice or experience the site in the same way.

Smith argues that exploring a problematic is a crucial shift for IE. Instead of identifying a theoretical stance or cultural condition in advance of the inquiry, "what will be brought under ethnographic scrutiny unfolds as the research is pursued" (Smith 2005, 34). Campbell and Gregor (2002, 7) refer to problematics similarly as social "puzzles"; as they explain, "someone is living the situation that you want to learn more about . . . the world is organized as it is for some purpose" (2002, 47–48). Thinking of the sites we study as complex, dynamic, flexible, multifaceted, layered, and shape-shifting in relation to our interests reaffirms that some practices within institutions will always be scripted for individuals but that individuals will also actively negotiate these points of institutional contact in highly personal and unique ways. A problematic may be captured in a single question, but the question itself must speak to the relationships the ethnographer hopes to explore. During the analysis of data, the institutional ethnographer can read problematics for the ways they expose an overlap of competing ideals and values or as sites where discourse and the particularities of lived experience refuse and resist one another. In a study of the status of contingent faculty, then, a researcher might explore how someone hired into a contingent line experiences the institutional sites in which they carry out their work or how they make decisions about what and how to teach. Individual narratives of experience—the everyday experience of particular sets of material conditions within a writing program, for instance—often give voice to moments of disjunction or misalignment that can be explored for the tensions they expose.

Work and Work Processes

> *Situations (contexts) do not just exist. Situations are rarely static or uniform, they are actively created, sustained, negotiated, resisted, and transformed moment by moment through ongoing work.*
>
> —James Paul Gee, "The New Literacy Studies: From 'Socially Situated' to the Work of the Social"

When people negotiate institutional processes, putting time and energy into the activities of a local setting, institutional ethnographers refer to this as "work." One of the many shifts entailed in IE scholarship is a turn to a broadly inclusive construct of "work." Where writing studies literature has largely been concerned with "labor"—contingent labor, faculty labor, the intellectual labor of program directors and administrators, or whether the work of the professionals in the field should be called "labor" at all (Marshall 2003)—Bruce Horner (2000, 92–93) explains how "work" can encompass more than just paid labor:

> Work, while encompassing labor, also includes activities . . . other than those for which one is paid (my "real work" to which I devote myself when not "at work"). Labor once also encompassed the general sense of social activity (Williams, Keywords 177): in Marx's terms, "an activity which adapts material for some purpose or other . . . a natural condition of human existence, a condition of material interchange between man [*sic*] and nature, quite independent of the forms of society" (Marx, Contribution 36), with "material" understood to include all forms of interchange, relations, and production that take place, whether recognized or valued by dominant ideology or not.

These definitions allow for a recognition of the mutually constitutive nature of writing and work in its many forms, as it is conducted by many different people within our studies. As Gee, Brandt, and others have argued extensively, writing plays a significant role in creating, maintaining, and organizing work. Writing is the vehicle of many work processes, from university mission statements; to college, department, and program websites; to correspondence between administrative units on a campus; to the syllabi faculty use in their classes, the forms and websites we use to teach classes, the handouts we compose to guide and inform students, and the comments we place on student written work. Writing is a series of practices that allows for the coordination of activities in different settings, at different times, and through the work of different people.

Much recent IE research has focused on the "front line" of public-sector employee work, with the concept of "work" defined very generously. Because the term is so inclusive, it is somewhat difficult to define, but Alison I. Griffith and Dorothy Smith (2014, 10) note that "in those institutional settings where services are provided to clients, we should remember that, using the 'generous' conception of work, those who are served are also working; they put in time and energy and are active in actual local settings as they engage with or are caught up in an institutional process."

More generally, Smith (2005, 229) uses the term *work* to refer to "anything that people do that takes time, effort, and intent." As an analytic lens that focuses writing researchers on what people do, "work" is one site where the actualities of experience and practice can be readily traced in the interplay between individual and broader systems of value.

DeVault (2008, 6) explains that work *processes* are "organizational strategies . . . [that] highlight and support some kinds of work while leaving other tasks unacknowledged, to be done without recognition, support, or any kind of collective responsibility." These processes ground the work of multiple individuals in conceptions of practice, providing the opportunity for the writing researcher to trace individual and institutional values in action. These "distinctive relational sequences"—*or how work gets done*—reveal the ways local cooperative efforts respond to and re-inscribe broader economies of value (Smith 2005, 54). Inquiry into how work processes come into being—who determines what will happen and how—reveals the influences, hierarchies, and organizing factors at work on individuals as they go about their daily activities. The process of undergoing an annual review is an excellent example of the power of work processes: individuals must fill out particular forms (typically approved in advance by the HR office), with very particular types of information to be included. The types of information included on the forms will often index closely to the individual's institutional rank, professional affiliation, or employment category. Not all work an individual will do in a given academic year will necessarily fit these categories. These forms are then submitted for review to a supervisor or committee (depending on the local protocol), and the individual's work is evaluated against a number of pre-established (and sometimes hidden) factors and criteria. Each of these steps is typically highly prescribed so the employer is in alignment with state employment laws, local culture, and expectations. The process must repeat in very similar ways across all employees with an institutional rank or category, or the employer risks accusations of unfair or capricious treatment.

Of course, this does not mean these processes are always transparent, fair, or clear. The relationships individuals may have with these processes are crucial to note because these relationships will reveal the components of experience: the personal philosophies, motives, and mutable practices that may give a location a particular character. We can understand "work" (in a classroom, in a hallway, in an office with a student), then, as both a social collaboration and a product of uniquely personal understandings, preferences, identifications, and affiliations with and within particular institutions, disciplines, and professional identities.

Each of these interdependent terms related to the activities and practices people carry out as they go about their work focuses the institutional ethnographer on powerful indicators of hierarchy, authority, and belonging within systems of work and labor, as these social forces coordinate the practices of unique individuals across space and time.

Institutional Discourse, Texts, Textual Mediation, and Boss Texts (Institutional Circuits)

Organizations coordinate any number of individuals over time and space and use written and visual texts in many forms to do so. From name badges, to email communications, to formal written policies, to complex procedures entailing textual notations, texts transmit ruling relations between sites—carrying rhetorical influence, granting agency and authority, casting representations of people and their work, and sanctioning activities. As Smith (2001, 160) writes, formalized discourse and texts have an "architectural significance" within organizations. "Institutional discourse," like the broader category of "ideological discourse," operates at meta-levels to control other discourses within an institutional site, creating generalizations and therefore a sense of continuity across individuals, practices, and sites (Smith 2005, 225).

IE's emphasis on texts "emerges from empirical observation as well as from theory; it comes from the insight that technologies of social control are increasingly and pervasively textual and discursive" (DeVault 2008, 6). Texts—such as organization and program websites, syllabi, the chapters in textbooks, rubrics, and textually mediated tools, like Blackboard or Moodle—can dramatically order conceptions of writing and student writers, enabling and constraining the faculty who teach writing classes, what their students do, and other elements of a site of writing. These examples demonstrate how texts mediate institutional discourse, regulating and authorizing the practices that are taken up by individuals.

The power of texts particularly arises out of their replicablity—they persist over time and space—and exhibits a seemingly fixed nature. As Smith (2001, 160) writes: "Texts and documents make possible the appearance of the same set of words, numbers or images in multiple local sites, however differently they may be read and taken up. They provide for the standardized recognizability of people's doings as organizational or institutional as well as for their co-ordination across multiple local settings and times."

"Boss texts," texts that carry authority "in such a way that an institutional course of action can follow" (Griffith and Smith 2014, 12), are of particular importance to the institutional ethnographer. As texts carry ideas, language, and rhetorical frameworks between individuals (even those with little personal interaction) to impose notions of ideal practice and affiliation, the texts are not just sources of information but shapers of thinking and practice. Likewise, through texts and textual practices, individuals are enabled to recognize, organize, and respond to processes of social coordination. "Boss texts" act particularly as forms of "institutional circuits," which create ideals of accountability, professionalism, and disciplinarity, as they regulate—and often standardize—practice, mediating idiosyncrasies and variability in local settings. Returning to the example of the annual review, the blank template produced by the HR office and used by departments to evaluate employees is an excellent example of an institutional circuit. More particular to writing studies, we might think of rubrics as the quintessential institutional circuit, especially those developed and designed to help create cohesion between the teaching practices and student works generated within a writing program. The terms on the rubric focus the teaching-work of faculty and students in visible ways, making the teaching that faculty provide accountable to the goals of a program and students accountable to the learning of the class.

Institutional discourses and documents may dramatically mediate our professional lives, producing often well-scripted relationships with and within the institution. Documents may prescribe understandings of our roles and our jobs, suggesting and contractually outlining the expectations for our daily and long-term practices. Institutional documents determine when our work year and workday begin and end, the size of our standard teaching loads, what constitutes an effectively active research agenda, guidelines for tenure and promotion, and other elements of our work. A simple distinction between teaching faculty and research faculty (a larger process of identification that begins with a literal notation on a piece of paper) can make an enormous difference in the institutional visibility, mobility, and access to resources for an individual. Texts such as faculty handbooks, HR regulations, and departmental bylaws may define the people and services to which an individual has access, the shape of their workday or year, and many other material factors in their work lives—whether they have an office, access to a photocopier, the ability to use departmental processes, recognition for their efforts, and more. A document such as an annual review or a time card orders and discursively represents our institutional experiences in key ways. These texts are so rolled up in the nature of our institutions that it is easy to take the work they do for granted, overlooking their significance for the ways they organize us into our institutional sites.

But the power of texts is also limited. Individuals must *actively* take up the discourses a text presents. In Smith's (2005, 105) words, a "text-reader conversation . . . brings the text into action *in* the readers who activate it." In IE, this process of activation is as unpredictable and dynamic as the individuals we study. Even texts that impose policy on a site, for instance, "trigger[ing] a complex of textually mediated activities," require activation by individuals and so can be misunderstood or refused (Nichols and Griffith 2009, 245). On the other hand, institutional ethnographers benefit from recognizing the organizational power and limitations of texts and institutional discourse, which can be rewritten, ignored, forgotten, or even lost or erased entirely.

These key terms demonstrate the ways an IE framework asks ethnographers to approach their research projects. The terms themselves are flexible, opening out in numerous ways and enabling the ethnographer to focus on the situated nature of experience and practice. Work with these terms and with the methodological awareness IE offers has the potential to extend and further develop many of the active critiques and discourses in writing studies, particularly concern for the material conditions of writing instruction. The terms open more extensive and explicit exploration of the ways work is carried out in writing classes, writing programs, and educational institutions and how we participate—sometimes unwittingly—in the co-constitution of institutional missions as we research, teach, learn, and administer sites of writing.

A small caution for those new to IE: those taking up IE will want to be careful about how their own understandings of terms may shape what they find within a site. As Smith (2001, 161) argues, understanding that our relations are materially and socially constituted is less about the imposition of a set of external tools or concepts that pre-conceptualize what the ethnographer may uncover; rather, these concepts can be used to flexibly explore and unpack the social relations and institutional circuits that shape what people are doing and how they are doing it. However, the terms themselves are useful only as they may help the ethnographer reveal the coordination of how things happen. That is, the institutional ethnographer's aim is to assemble the many different knowledges and understandings of experience and practice that filter throughout a site, bringing to light the stories that might otherwise be skipped over, elided, or erased by institutional discourses, conceptual categories, and the ways we name people, places, and practices. Smith (2005, 160) refers to this as "creating a map or model of that aspect of institutional organization." We might think of this as a representation of the institution as those who live and work within its rich contexts know it: "an empirical bridge between local and particular processes," which brings to light the ways individuals actively negotiate the "social relations that order everyday existence" (Luken and Vaughan 2005, 1604).

Getting a sense of the entirety of an institution is not always possible, of course. As such, the IE researcher might scale and target his or her work, pursuing particular strands of an institutional complex or the actualities that are circumscribed by active professional discussions. Smith and other institutional ethnographers recommend thinking of the narratives produced by IE as complementary; alone they may tell only a sliver of a larger story, but together they flesh out the dynamic workings of a much larger social order: "Each next step builds from what has been discovered and [details] more extended dimensions of the institutional regime. The mapping of social relations expands from and includes the original site so that the larger organization that enters into and shapes it becomes visible" (Smith 2005, 35). With each tightly focused project (scaled to time lines and available resources), we build upon what we have already known and established, finding new perspectives to explore and developing a more expansive understanding of how our work plays out in everyday contexts for real people. As we continue to think about how work with IE brings new stories to light for the field of writing studics, institutional ethnographers must continue to think about how projects using IE can extend and deepen already ongoing conversations about our work within sites of writing. As a framework for research, IE offers exciting possibilities that will carry ethnographers and their research contributions in new and necessary directions.

The following chapters show IE in action. Each of the following case studies explores a problematic, uncovering the chemistry among ruling relations, standpoints, experience, and practice within three unique sites of interest to writing studies researchers. As a field struggling with the ways the age of austerity, the rise of institutional accountability, and the increasingly neoliberal contexts of employment and labor in higher education persistently complicate our daily work, we have much to gain from the shifts in attention, questioning, and systematic analysis that IE offers. The framework's vocabulary and analytics offer new ways to study the actualities of our work lives. As professionals in writing studies are increasingly called upon to explain how institutional contexts are impacting our work, our programs, and the results of our applied disciplinary knowledge, we can use IE and similar tools to show the actualities of our relationships among writing, writers, and local materialities. IE provides a complex research apparatus that allows us to more effectively study the pressing and swiftly changing actualities of our work lives.

2

HOW WORK TAKES SHAPE

Tracing the Work of a "Shared Assignment" in a Linked Gateway

English 202: *Introduction to the Study of English Language and Literature*

Gateway course designed for English pre-majors and majors. Introduces critical, historical, and theoretical frameworks important to studying the literature, language, and cultures of English. Concurrent registration with ENGL 197 required.

English 197: *Interdisciplinary Writing/Humanities*

Expository writing based on material presented in a specified humanities lecture course. Assignments include drafts of papers to be submitted in the specified course, and other pieces of analytical prose. Concurrent registration in the specified course required.

—University of Washington
Course Catalog, 2007

* * *

Major Essay 1: Working from Your Close Readings to a Critical Reading of Munro's *The Love of a Good Woman*

We will spend the early days of this course closely accounting for what we observe and the responses that accompany those observations when we read Alice Munro's The Love of a Good Woman. We will work closely with individual passages, noting which elements capture our attention (uses of language, representations of actions, settings, or character, a narrative voice or perspective that accompanies those representations) and the responses they elicit in us as readers (visceral, emotional, moral, or intellectual). We will also tease out connections among passages and explore the role such connections play in our experience of the work and its meaning.

Major Essay 1 will grow out of the short writings you generate through close reading of The Love of a Good Woman. In the essay you will analyze three to four passages you see as forming a thread or a larger complex significant to the meaning of the work. In your paper, then, you will produce an interpretation of the text informed by the sum of your encounters with

DOI: 10.7330/9781607328667.c002

the work. Serious students of literary texts recognize this production—the generation of an interpretation after a sustained grappling with a text—as an important intellectual process that prepares them to engage in larger critical debates about a work.

A strong essay will show readers how elements of the passages you analyze come together to create important effects and meanings within the story. In arguing for connectivity among the passages, a convincing paper will demonstrate the particular contributions of each passage without reducing them to mere examples of the same phenomenon.

4 to 5 pages double spaced.

* * *

A writing assignment tells a story of work. Writing assignments are produced by real people, as a means to negotiate national, local, and personal ideals of writing, writers, and the work of writing instruction. As such, writing assignments sit at the interstices of institutional being, indexing the moments in which labor, expertise, professional identity, local norms, and material conditions come together to influence what we do. As "situated point[s] of entry" (LaFrance and Nicolas 2012, 151) into the complex processes of decision-making, ideals of authority, and routine that constitute our work as writing teachers, writing assignments have much to teach us about how the field's ideals of pedagogy take material shape.

In this chapter I trace the collaborative development of shared writing assignments in a series of "linked" courses developed to introduce undergraduates to the work of the English major at a large R1 university on the West Coast.[1] This curricular initiative, referred to in this chapter as the "linked gateway," connected a large lecture (about the critical, historical, and theoretical frameworks for the study of literature—conceptualized as a curricular "gateway" to study in the English major) with a series of smaller writing courses (typically referred to as "links") that drew their content from the large lecture. Studying the collaborative design of shared assignments in the linked gateway serves two purposes in this chapter and the larger project of this book. The first goal is to explicitly outline the moves central to doing institutional ethnography (IE), using the development of shared assignments to demonstrate the key analytic approaches of the institutional ethnographer in action and to show how findings are discovered in an IE project. The second goal is to uncover the story of work underwriting the development of shared writing assignments in a hierarchical but collaborative setting, a story that opens for deeper understanding the ways material actualities (such as patterns of labor, disciplinary identity, and ideals of writing instruction) coordinated the work of the site.

Many aspects of this story will be familiar to those who have studied labor conditions in the field or linked-course initiatives. As an example of the ways IE allows us to study how our work takes shape, the story told here offers a sense of the power of the methodology to turn up particularities that are highly relevant to the concerns of writing program administrators but often less visible in the scholarship of curricular initiatives and WAC/WID work. Identifying the fuller picture of what is actually happening in the sites where we carry out work allows us—as researchers—to better understand the nature of the personal investments of those we work with and expands opportunities for us to recognize, innovate with, and intervene in how that work is taking its shape. The findings of this study particularly push on our most active understandings of "pedagogy" in the field of writing studies, specifically the pedagogical discourses of writing program administration and WAC/WID initiatives.

As Michael W. Apple (2004, 17) notes, curricular initiatives are ideology in action; courses and their designs follow established social patterns, acting as "filters" for knowledge, cultural capital, economic utility, and the legitimization of hierarchical social relations. They are sites where "the *interplay* between cultural knowledge" and "the stuff we teach" reveals "the extant economic and political forms which now provide the principles upon which so much of our everyday lives are [*sic*] organized" (Apple 2004, 40, original emphasis). An institutional ethnography of a collaborative endeavor like the linked gateway, however, reveals that if curricular initiatives are ideological, they are also undeniably material: ideals of disciplinary identity, prestige and certification, labor relations, and expertise cannot truly be separated from epistemologies, shared understandings of doing and knowing, and the dynamic shape of writing instruction.

As professionals and the members of professional organizations, we often speak of pedagogy in a generalized or theoretical sense—discussing broad teaching strategies (such as teaching for transfer, writing about writing, disciplinary writing, critical pedagogies authoring national standards and policy, and arguing for some approaches over others based on ideals of student learning). This study, with its grounding in the IE framework, shows us an altogether different picture; when "pedagogy" plays out within local contexts, we begin to see how the material relations of a site shape and reshape the generative work of the idealized intervention—often in ways that belie or disregard the values and practices at the center of the original ideal. In a local sense, then, pedagogy appears as a *highly individualized and material process* that organizes the particularities of work around fairly particular sets of values.

Institutional ethnographers use the term *work* to refer to "anything that people do that takes time, effort, and intent" (Smith 2005, 229). As an analytic lens that focuses writing researchers on how people negotiate the everyday, "work" is a significant site for understanding the actualities of experience and practice that live below professional and disciplinary discourses. Tracing the development of an assignment can reveal a good deal about the granularities of work within a writing program, classroom, or teaching initiative. Work processes, like the production of assignments, make visible "organizational strategies . . . [that] highlight and support some kinds of work while leaving other tasks unacknowledged, to be done without recognition, support, or any kind of collective responsibility" (DeVault 2008, 6). The "distinctive relational sequences"—or *how work gets done*—negotiated in these interactions reveal the ways local cooperative efforts respond to and re-inscribe broader economies of value, including labor and other professional inequities (Smith 2005, 54).

The linked gateway courses are an ideal background for this demonstration since, unlike "hermetically sealed" (Graff 2009) standalone courses, the highly collaborative nature of the gateway brings into relief work processes and relationships that are far more difficult to see when carried out in the comfortable isolation of the traditional classroom. All teachers of writing, indeed, all faculty, are negotiating their understandings of professional standards, ideals of learning, and local values when they carry out the work of writing instruction. But since "linked" (also "paired," or "combined") courses share students and some elements of syllabi, readings, writing assignments, and teaching objectives (LaFrance 2010), the interconnected curricular opportunities they provide make visible many of the processes of decision-making, institutional and professional alignment, and resource investment that are often elided, ignored, or erased in isolated classroom settings.

Moreover, because linked courses have been critiqued for the ways they re-inscribe the labor and professional inequities of today's institutions of higher education (Kirsch 1988; Luebke 2002; LaFrance 2010), they offer us an understanding of the actualities underpinning many curricular initiatives in hierarchical environments. Those teaching linked courses must often collaborate across sometimes fairly different material relations, negotiating differing professional statuses, institutional ranks and identities, types of professional experience, and teaching philosophies. Linked-course initiatives may bring rather different types of pedagogical practice and disciplinary content together—a factor that may complicate seamless understandings of what faculty would like students to learn and do. Yet the collaborative nature of the "link" requires that faculty find points of commonality, building some moments of continuity, however small, into the work of both courses. The resulting conversations and negotiations can reveal the numerous disjunctions and tensions that are common to, but also commonly hidden in, the experience and practice of writing instruction as work.

The linked gateway of this study was no exception to the fraught norms of labor organization that have marked the institutionalization of writing studies labor more generally. As the course descriptions in this chapter's epigraph demonstrate, *English 202: Introduction to the Study of English Language and Literature* was instituted as a five-credit, large lecture that exposed students to critical, historical, and theoretical frameworks active within the field of English studies. These courses were taught by senior literature faculty who had received tenure in the department and were known as notable literary scholars in a sub-field of English studies. A five-credit course in its own right, *English 197: A Writing-Link with English 202* continued the conversations of English 202 and supported students as they composed and revised three or more major writing assignments during the quarter. The writing links were taught by non-tenure-track lecturers in the Interdisciplinary Writing Program (IWP) and English department teaching assistants.[2] The collaborative *and* hierarchical nature of the linked gateway required consistent negotiation of work processes, from schedules and routines to agreements about the critical frames (and therefore the resulting pedagogical approaches) assignments entailed.

Uncovering the collaborative development of writing assignments allows us to see how the institution took shape through the work of the gateway, making visible the sanctioned and unsanctioned (or underground) moments of teaching, identity, and professional belonging central to many sites of interest to writing studies scholars. This study's findings subsequently push on the ways pedagogy and labor are frequently conceived of as distinct from one another in the field of writing studies. We often represent pedagogy as a series of generalized conceptual moves that organize our own work and the work of others; my work reveals instead that pedagogy, in a local sense, is often more process than concept, more individualized than generalized, and more closely imbricated with materialities than we typically acknowledge in our field's discourses. Moreover, as this chapter serves the additional purpose of modeling how to carry out a project with IE, the background study serves to demonstrate how the fundamental practices of an institutional ethnographer reveal and contextualize the layers of experience and practice that constitute a site.

DOING IE: BUILDING EMPIRICAL BRIDGES

I will break briefly from the story of the linked gateway to continue and extend the previous chapter's conversation about how we do IE. When institutional ethnographers ask "how are things happening here?" we stretch beyond the recognition that social interactions are structured through powerful and at times coercive forces to seek an understanding of how actual people negotiate the factors that most enable, constrain, enliven, or direct their work. To begin this process of re-seeing the institution, the institutional ethnographer uncovers the relational nature of a site, "looking up" from a particular standpoint to see how work takes its shape from that vantage point. Multiple experiences and practices are then assembled through the course of a study to present a complex and dynamic understanding of how the institution is co-constituted. The institution is recognized as a site of dialogic and multi-vocal belongings. The practices studied, such as the construction of writing assignments, handouts, and other teaching artifacts, are read as moments of negotiation, where actual people make visible their unique understandings of the institution and their roles within it.

While there is no one way to do IE, Ursula T. Wright and Tonette S. Rocco (2016, 28) note that IE projects generally unfold in two stages. The first stage requires "fully understanding and developing the research [p]roblematic" by getting a sense of the contradictions and disjunctions of lived experience that are central to a particular set of social interactions. I have previously referred to this process of "looking up" (Smith 2006, 5) as building "an empirical bridge between local and particular processes" in order to bring to light the ways individuals actively negotiate the "social relations that order everyday existence" (Luken and Vaughan 2005, 1604). Shari Brotman (2000, 109) describes this process more succinctly as establishing a "gaze on the macro structure from the micro level," such that the problematic and standpoint that anchor an IE project may be recognized as closely related starting points in the larger unfolding of a project. If a problematic is a situation that will yield the disjunctions present in lived experience, a standpoint is the heuristic that orients an institutional ethnographer to the particularities of that experience. In the case of the study of English 202 and English 197, the problematic was a concern for how the work of writing assignments was coordinated within the collaborative yet hierarchical environment of the gateway. While I pay close attention to aspects of the TA experience in some areas of this chapter, I chose not to focus on one anchor standpoint alone—such as focusing primarily on the literature faculty, writing faculty, or IWP faculty. Instead, my overall project focuses on the story of work and work processes that emerged from the experience and practice of all participants in my study.

Stage two for an IE project, according to Wright and Rocco, entails the process of data gathering, which must draw from the many layers of institutional discourse and seek out ways to map (or document) individual experience. Stage two often begins with assembling official and public documents and securing permission to use these documents in the course of research. In pressing to represent a range of institutional perspectives, the researcher seeks to read widely about the formal nature of the site, paying close attention to how these documents represent the work of the site, those who carry out that work, and any issues that may be public knowledge. Once official documents have been secured and read for context, the institutional ethnographer will then seek to collect more personal and experiential accounts, interviews about experience, descriptions of practice, observations of key activities, and harder-to-find documents that are not necessarily "public," such as notes, email communications, and other artifacts offered by participants. Interviews, observations, and participation in the site are the keys to generating deeper understandings of relationships, processes, and social interactions; moreover, these interactions must be deliberately geared toward uncovering experiences and practices that are hidden by the official or sanctioned narratives, which are intended to give a site its most public identity.

In my study of how assignments took shape in the linked gateway, for instance, data collection included not just published statements, such as catalog descriptions and syllabi of the gateway courses, but also less formal public documents that set departmental conversations to record: the department's most recent self-study (part of a ten-year review), the minutes of the curriculum committee's discussion of the linked gateway courses, the particular course descriptions for each iteration of the course, assessment results, TA course files on record with the Interdisciplinary Writing Program, and an internal study conducted by the university's Office of Institutional Research to aid the department in its ongoing conversations about the learning goals of the course. I supplemented these examples of institutional discourse with private interviews with a number of departmental stakeholders and those who worked in different areas of the collaboration. As I explain in more detail below, I structured all of my interviews to ask explicitly about how interviewees envisioned their work in the gateway, how they were invited to participate in the collaboration, how they understood the goals of the courses, what they did in their own classes, and how they experienced some of the challenges of the collaboration.

Each IE project entails an ongoing and recursive development of an analytic framework, a process of thinking about how the key terms of chapter 1—ruling relations, standpoint, social coordination, problematic, work and work processes, and institutional circuits—lend focus to what the institutional ethnographer sees unfolding through his or her research practice. Social relations and the forces that coordinate our work—values, identities, and preferred practices—can be sifted from documents but are also often revealed in the ways participants answer questions. Interviews and observations offer new information about experience and practice and may confirm areas of overt or passive resistance. Reading across datasets, analysis will slowly reveal how people do what they do. The goal is to uncover the moments of difference (disjunctions) that may have been previously erased, elided, or ignored. In this project, for instance, a first round of analysis of the department's documents about the linked gateway uncovered that faculty did not agree on the learning goals for the lecture course; in subsequent reading and interviews, issues of workload, communication, and divisions of labor became more clear.

IE recasts traditional understandings of data triangulation as well. As Wright and Rocco (2016, 33) explain: "Realizing that informants' talk was shaped by something, institutional ethnographers consult texts to develop a concrete understanding of the experiential account that the informant explained in contrast and comparison to the actualities of what is really happening. The purpose is not to validate data, but to extend the researcher's understanding of what is taking place. Important to this phase of data collection and analysis is the notion that power is carried through the ideological constructs of texts. Analysis is about deriving particular meaning from the data as to their social construction across multiple settings."

To say this a little differently, the institutional ethnographer reads not for facts (though facts may indeed play a role in the final research narrative) but for a dynamic and composite understanding of experiences and practices at a site. Reading across texts, interviews, observations, and other available data, the institutional ethnographer slowly builds an understanding of how people do what they do, a process of negotiating their work into being.

"LOOKING UP FROM WHERE YOU ARE": STARTING WITH A TA STANDPOINT

> *From my own courses and from what I hear from other TAs, teaching 197/202 is the most time consuming [of the] courses that I have taught as a TA. I frequently went over 20 hours per week and came out in the end well above the quarterly limit.*
>
> —TA 18 (IWP course file)

As I note in chapter 1, the institutional ethnographer seeks to uncover the unique perspectives, attitudes, or positions of individuals, recognizing that the way an individual must be in the world is often highly prescribed. This situated uniqueness—what feminist theorists call standpoint—is understood as the embodiment of our knowledge, experience, and the ways we identify. What we think of as individual characteristics are as much products of historical, cultural, and social values and beliefs as they are personal choices. Identifying a standpoint within the site of study allows an institutional ethnographer to explore that location and its problematics with fresh eyes—seeking to understand how the institution and work take their shape from that distinctive situation in time and space. A focus on a standpoint, for instance, may uncover tensions, disjunctions, and erasures that looking at a site from a different angle will not expose.

I began my exploration of the particularities of work in the linked gateway by focusing on the standpoint of TAs. I began here for a very particular reason: while they were often the people least responsible for the gateway's design (such as the selection of readings, development of learning activities, and establishment of schedules), of all participants, TAs often had the most experience with the gateway because they would teach differing iterations of the writing links from quarter to quarter with different literature faculty leading the large lecture and different lead IWP faculty coordinating the work of the writing links. These return experiences allowed TAs to have a comparative sense of the gateway's many processes and players. Their ability to reflect on differences and similarities over time was very helpful for gaining a sense of the ruling relations of the site. In fact, many TAs had very strong opinions about the work of the gateway and how it took shape, offering the most information about the processes that resulted in writing assignments and other instructional activities.

I want to focus here on a portion of a longer interview with one of my most outspoken TA participants, because the TA's responses provide crucial insights into the collaborative efforts that shaped participants' work on the linked gateway courses and demonstrate the power of IE, particularly the ways standpoint and ruling relations may be exposed in the same moments of talk about work. In the section of our interview shared below, TA #8 has responded to a question I raised about the process of developing the writing assignments for the linked gateway. I offer a section of this transcript below (leaving it largely complete). In addition, I have underlined those portions of TA #8's response that seem to reveal information relevant to this chapter's dual conversation about the key terms of IE in action *and* the work of writing assignments in the linked gateway. These underlined elements serve the double purpose of highlighting what captured my attention as an ethnographer and offering a sense of the narrative points that informed my ongoing study of the work of the gateway. To offer explicit modeling around the analytic moves of IE, I have inserted notes (as right-justified blocks of text) to demonstrate how the institutional ethnographer teases out the key analytics of IE in informant responses. At the end of the transcript, I offer further discussion of how this interview supports a situated understanding of work processes in the linked gateway. Later sections of this chapter turn to other aspects of IE to flesh out the larger story of work to be told.

Interview with TA #8

> **TA8 (personal interview):** There was an agenda that we got on the first day; we didn't stick to it so closely. We talked a little bit about the evolution of the class. Not a whole lot. And a lot of people in the room had some 202 experience already or were already 197 instructors. So there was maybe only one person who had no knowledge of the class before. <u>Mostly, we looked at the course packet for 202 this quarter. We looked at that and the course description and the course calendar.</u>
>
> > **Researcher's note:** It seems telling that the initial topic of conversation in the meeting was the course pack, the course description, and the calendar. I see ruling relations making themselves visible here—as the priorities suggest the authority of the literature faculty. This is understandable—the center of both courses would be the shared reading—but also interesting as the entire process is put into place by the literature faculty member who designs the lecture. In this response, the TA seems to be suggesting that all other processes originate from that initial design/move. This is definitely a compelling statement about how work processes came to some shape.
>
> **TA8 (*continued*):** And [the lead IWP faculty] sort of gave us the breakdown of the three sequences and the ways we would be following the class and the ways we wouldn't. I had a lot of questions and probably harped on

him a bit too much regarding the relationship between 202 and 197, but those—you know, those questions came up and went down again. We talked mostly about: How did the sequences break down? What is the relationship between the two courses? What am I responsible for teaching? That was a big question that came up for me.

> **Researcher's note:** The TA is clearly speaking here about work processes as he understands them. The TA notes being given the shared "sequences" (a term often used interchangeably for the writing assignments); these have been developed by the lead IWP faculty. The TA notes that the group spoke together about some expectations for the teaching of the writing links—what to focus on, what to leave to the lectures. This is an interesting nod to the ongoing conversations about divisions of labor that structured the two courses. The conversation then turns to logistics, interactions, and responsibility. Power and authority seem to be a significant, if unacknowledged, presence in the process(es) discussed—the TA standpoint suggested in this interview seems to be positioned outside of that authority.

ML: What are you responsible for teaching?

TA8: Ummmm . . . I decided to eventually answer that on my own. I don't think I understood initially the level or the limits of my autonomy. To what extent did I get to make decisions versus [the lead IWP faculty] versus [the lead literature faculty]? And that was something that I just recently in the last two weeks really figured out. On the one hand, they give us the major paper prompts and an overview of what the sequence is going to be . . . which we have to rewrite because the major paper prompts are incredibly vague and draw numerous complaints from students who don't understand them.

> **Researcher's note:** This quotation reads to me very much as if the TA is tracing how authority works in the gateway—as this TA discusses "limits," the roles of others, and what he himself must figure out, we're seeing a series of the tensions he is experiencing as he tries to distinguish his work from the work of others and the shape his work will take as he works with his students. This strikes me as a strong indicator of standpoint. It seems that one of the biggest issues in shaping the work of the gateway is that people don't share a sense of how to develop an assignment—should an assignment be developed to reflect what we know about process in writing courses, to focus on some shared pedagogical goals, to make explicit critical moves in English studies, or for some other reason? In this conversation, these goals do not seem to be integrated.

TA8 (*continued*): The other problem is that we generated the first major paper prompt four days before the class began, and that was very stressful—because everybody in that room had come out of the composition program and we were taught to scaffold toward the major paper. So, you start with the major paper and you have a week to figure out how you're going to teach.

> **Researcher's note:** Another tension is revealed in this interview response. The TAs teaching the writing links have all been trained (in the TA training class) and have worked substantially in their own, autonomous composition classrooms. Teaching writing as a process is a norm in the composition program, so it is rote for TAs to break each major paper into smaller pieces, "scaffolding" the work asked of students and going slowly over key elements of college-level writing. Most of the literature faculty have not had such extensive experience in composition classrooms and so are unfamiliar with the norms of teaching writing (as it is imagined in composition). Faculty understandings of teaching writing and the TAs' understanding of teaching writing are at times, then, at odds. (TAs are used to having their schedules determined by process, not by a reading list or other course structures.) So while TAs are used to very regularized and slow schedules for assignments, the literature faculty also have a different sensibility about how to compose a course schedule. When these situated experiences and their related understandings of teaching are unpacked, it is easy to see that TAs often struggle to teach in ways that are familiar, as they subsequently manage other, often newer, concerns—this realization is clearly about work processes and a conflict in assumptions about how those processes will be determined.

TA8 ***(continued)*****:** And for us—we didn't have that time. We had to just inductively do it. We didn't understand the major prompts because we ourselves didn't come up with them. We hadn't yet had the opportunity to do the reading for the course. And so the first sequence for a lot of people was kind of taking it in day by day, doing some close readings, and then figuring out what the first sequence was going to be about and then working backward until you got to the present day.

> **Researcher's note:** A clear disjunction is identified here. This response suggests that work as it is framed by the literature faculty creates a series of practical issues for TAs; the exigencies of the linked gateway collaboration then shape TA work as a response to those issues over a move toward a shared pedagogical center. This TA feels it is very important to "understand" the writing assignments to be taught—likely, this has to do with other aspects of writing instruction that are well outside the line of vision of the literature faculty. It seems very much like the literature faculty and the TAs are operating under quite different professional ideals about what teaching writing entails. This is clearly standpoint in action. The TA's discussion of the strategy, that is, "taking it day by day" and "working backward," is a clear reference to work processes as they are shaped by the ruling conditions (relations) of the gateway.

> **TA8** ***(continued)*****:** I'm not comfortable with that role because it seems contrary to everything I've been taught as the basis of proper or productive pedagogy. And so it's very hard for me to have an undefined role. What is the goal of my class if I'm not allowed to set those goals? And if I am allowed to set those goals, to what degree can I diverge from [the goals established by the literature and IWP faculty]?
>
> > **Researcher's note:** The questions the TA asks have an urgency. Without a clear sense of personal purpose and focus, it may be difficult for TAs to make decisions about how they will do what they will do. I see this as a discussion of experience and therefore closely related to standpoint.
>
> **TA8** ***(continued)*****:** There was a real difference between the veteran 197 instructors and the first-timers. People like me who were trying to reconcile the system with what they want to do and people who had done it before, who are clearly just doing whatever they're doing. I mean, I get the sense that there is a lot of off-book teaching. And no one really talks about it so much. I don't know the extent of that. I wouldn't say that I rewrote the paper prompt for the second sequence. But I would say that I heavily revised it. And it does the same thing, but it is worded very differently. And my sequence was different.
>
> > **Researcher's note:** Here the informant is suggesting that TAs end up making decisions in ways that make sense to them but may not take those decisions back to the larger group. So the work processes of the gateway, if we read this TA at face value, impose a sense of authority and autonomy for some but not for all. I will need to look into how these moments of coordination play out in the broader contexts of the linked gateway. Revising the writing assignments and reworking the "sequences" may be one small indicator of a much larger underground sensibility. This admission troubles our ability to call writing assignments in the linked gateway "boss texts"—there's just too much slippage around practice to be certain about their power. Though it does make them appear as significant forms of "institutional circuitry," in that they offer up the ideals of standard practice that others can immolate. An interesting distinction.

As this TA narrates the work processes undergirding writing assignments in the gateway, he tells a story of relationships, authority, choices, and practice. This moment of informant confidence reveals a number of intriguing possibilities for further exploration in other interviews, observations, and texts. The line of inquiry I began to develop focused my next analytic moves (which here take the form of questions): Where did authority originate in the gateway? Was it safe to say official and unofficial work processes were involved in the work of the linked gateway? And if so, did they take shape differently? This informant suggested that logistics tended to be a concern for TAs (as they seem to be offered the least amount of time to organize a significant amount of teaching practice). Most important, the relationships at the center of the linked gateway seemed to influence to a good degree how work for everyone involved in the gateway would take shape.

With these possibilities established, my exploration of the gateway continued. I began to seek an understanding of the ruling relations of the site so that I could see the connections to individual experience and practice they might reveal. But even here, from a single interview, we can see the ways the pedagogical ideals of the gateway took on an uneasy tension with the material actualities of work for some of those involved in the linked gateway initiative. This example interview, then, reminds institutional ethnographers of the ways individuals will also negotiate ruling relations and other material actualities in highly unique ways, enacting an array of fairly different values from unique standpoints. As a starting point in an IE-based study, we can begin to feel out the edges of a problematic—the close, but often elided or disavowed, relationship between material conditions and pedagogy, for instance.

THE EXTRA-LOCAL IS ALSO LOCAL: THE RULING RELATIONS OF LABOR IN HIGHER ED AND CRISIS IN ENGLISH STUDIES

> *Smith saw the benefits of being able to make visible as social relations the complex practices that coordinate people's actions across separations of time and space, often without their conscious knowledge . . . Something is actually connecting what happens here to what happens there. The analysis shows social relations being realized in people's practices.*
>
> —Marie Campbell and Frances Gregor, *Mapping Social Relations: A Primer in Doing Institutional Ethnography*

A pause here as well to retrace and expand upon the discussion of ruling relations—"that extraordinary yet ordinary complex of relations . . . that connect us across space and time and organize our everyday lives" (Smith 2005, 10)—from chapter 1. Uncovering the complex constellation of ruling relations at any site begins with reading national and local contexts with and against the active stories of experience and practice that have been offered by participants or uncovered through observation—identifying the trends and patterns in stories that echo in different texts and accounts and across different sorts of experiences. Once these initial moments of co-constitution are identified, the ethnographer may also turn to a number of fairly broad institutional, popular, and disciplinary sources to "build empirical bridges" between the personal experiences they have uncovered and broader complexes of power, influence, and history. Because ruling relations are about how the local takes organizational shape in relation to extra-local discourses, including material conditions, professional standards, and key national conversations or patterns of social organization, the institutional ethnographer might turn to finding similar lines of thought in sources that have appeared in institutional, professional, and national venues. In some cases, the ethnographer need look no further than a faculty handbook, a union contract, a program website, or the communication that arises from a departmental or program leader to find a source that yields insights into key ruling relations. In other cases, the ruling relations that organize a site may be traced through a discussion of trends in higher education. Sometimes ruling relations are apparent in the popularity of topics in research journals and the publications of professional organizations. For other conversations, the ethnographer might wish to turn to public controversy or accounts that have appeared in the national or regional press to provide background and recognize active social investments within a professional or local community.

The linkage of a large lecture in English and a cluster of smaller writing courses brought together literature faculty, IWP faculty, and TAs in ways that were new for all involved, but the collaborative effort was yet the product of the persistent patterns of labor that structured the department. The development of a single introductory lecture (English 202) for the core curriculum was an intensive undertaking in its own right; few tenure-line faculty in English had taught large lecture courses previously, as the department had long held to the ideal of smaller, discussion-based courses. Similarly, few of the tenure-line literature faculty had taught in the ways an introductory course might require, stepping away from the hyperspecialization English studies has long been known for and meeting new students at the threshold of disciplinary study. Meanwhile, those who taught the writing links, both IWP faculty and the TAs, had a good deal of experience teaching students new to the university and the major. And even though the IWP is one of the longest running and most recognized linked writing course programs in the United States, its full-time faculty have traditionally held contingent lines, and the majority of its courses have been staffed with graduate students from English who were in the late stages of their PhD work. These graduate students had typically exhausted other forms of graduate funding on campus.

The economic standing of graduate students who taught in the gateway was at times rather perilous, though, like most inequities in the gateway, this material condition was rarely acknowledged. These conditions at times interfered with my ability to include TAs in the ongoing work of my study. Some held other jobs off campus. Others did not feel that talking about the linked gateway was of interest or in their personal interest. One of the graduate students I contacted for an interview, in fact, responded by email that she did not feel comfortable talking about the linked courses: it was "too much like biting the hand that feeds me." Another TA responded with a very honest confession about the pressures of her financial and familial obligations. "Sorry to take a while to respond!" she wrote:

> I'm a bit overwhelmed right now. I'm sorry—I really don't want to sit and talk about 197. I'm trying to figure out what to do with myself, thinking about adding on a part-time job, confused about school, wanting a real job, dealing with my kids, etc. It's a mess. Okay—hope to see you soon, in any case.

I include these responses here because they provide a crucial understanding of both social relations and the material actualities of the gateway. As an institutional ethnographer, I feel compelled to read the lived experience of precariousness as a major influence on TA work in general. Yet the power dynamic of the linked gateway required that these experiences, while central to the work of TAs, remain in the background, muted.

And here we see the power of ruling relations, as they reveal how extra-local discourses bear a close relationship to local experience and practice. (In other words, we see a collapse of macro and micro concerns.) As Marjorie L. DeVault (2008, 21) writes, neoliberal logics of work and labor have a double-ness: "recruit[ing] local actors to a reorganization of consciousness and thereby align[ing] their activity with ruling agendas. Empowerment through paid work, for example, may be understood in the context of an individual's life as a route to economic security, pride in accomplishment, and recognition as a full member of society. Within the managerial logic of the new economy, however, the same concept can refer to a stark version of independence in which individuals increasingly shoulder all the responsibilities and risks of their own and other's sustenance."

The scholarship of labor in writing studies has long recognized the devaluation of writing instruction in departments of English (especially when organized as a composition program or classroom) under these auspices; the "vexed disciplinary history" John Schilb (2002, 167) identifies in the labor contexts of writing studies undeniably makes itself felt in the TA experience of the linked gateway. Ironically, even as the teaching of writing provides the primary economic engine for English departments (J. Harris 2000) and has enabled (historically) the development of literary specialization, the values of English studies at large have relegated the teaching and study of writing instruction to a lower status than the teaching and study of literature. The linked-course arrangement allowed the department to meet several pedagogical and economic needs at once, and so the ideals of expertise, leadership, and work in relation to the linked gateway were entirely bound up with the material histories and the material relations within which these ideals were situated. These material actualities dramatically inflected the processes of collaboration and communication central to the work of writing assignments in the gateway, often determining whose authority, decisions, and vision would come to the fore as assignments took shape.

Another ruling relation further complicated the organization of the linked gateway and requires our attention as researchers: The literary faculty involved in developing the lecture disagreed about how the lecture should be organized. Was it a survey course? An introduction to some critical approaches active in the field (as time would not allow a meaningful introduction to all of the possible critical approaches)? An introduction to close reading? An exploration of the history of English studies? Or a treatment of the concept of disciplinarity? Each of these possible starting points and frames for the lecture made a dramatic difference in how the writing links would be designed as well.

Consider these interview responses, for example, each offered by a tenured faculty member in English who specialized in a literary field:

> **Tenured Literature Faculty 1:** How do you design an introduction to a discipline that is having an identity crisis? Part of the problem with this course—it's called the "gateway to the discipline," but the discipline is a mess! We're all standing within our own different relations to the discipline. And I'm sure some of my colleagues don't even think I'm in the discipline.
>
> * * *
>
> **Tenured Literature Faculty 2:** It's a discipline of contestation. Of the very meaning of the concept of discipline. It's a contestation of different ways of conceiving of the discipline and even of points of view that disavow the entire notion that English is a discipline. And that's a lot of what this course is about. And that's the whole nature of the postmodern condition . . .
>
> * * *
>
> **Tenured Literature Faculty 5:** What do we do when we do English studies? That's a very hard question to answer.
>
> * * *
>
> **Tenured Literature Faculty 6:** What if you don't believe in a coherent discipline?
>
> * * *

Consider as well this excerpt from a report on a study of the linked gateway conducted by an independent researcher from the Office of Educational Assessment:

> **To:** [Department Chair] and [Director, English Undergraduate Education]
> **From:** [Researcher] and [Researcher], Office of Educational Assessment
> **Subject:** Focus Groups: English 202/197 Students
> **Date:** June 20, 2007
>
> This memo provides a report of those focus groups as part of the broader assessment of the English 202/197 linked gateway to the major.
>
> What do you see as the strengths in requiring the linked ENGL 202/197 for English majors?
>
> There was no agreement about the strengths of requiring English 202/197 across the three focus groups. Students in each group noted that the English 202/197 course was a good requirement because it:
>
> - Serves as a prerequisite to start students off in the major ("It's the one time you have everyone together and you can teach the foundation of what every English major should know—a valuable opportunity.")
> - Provides a good introduction to English 302
> - Teaches close reading and literary periods
> - Introduces writing in the major, particularly important to transfer students
> - Gives hope to English majors about the range of opportunities ahead
> - Makes use of interesting guest lecturers

In this portion of the report there was not agreement among those stakeholders (from three different focus groups) interviewed about whether the course should be a *requirement or a prerequisite* for study in the major; however, *students* interviewed noted a number of possible contributions to their learning on which the course could capitalize. This range of opinion across stakeholders was a reflection of the uncertainties of many faculty in English studies, which then trickled into and fed the confusions exposed here as well.

Like the ruling relations of labor, faculty confusions about what practices best prepared undergraduates entering the major were a dynamic reflection of broader national conversations in the field of English studies. What we call "English," according to Bruce McComiskey (2006), is an administrative structure suturing together a number of fields and subfields with their own professional journals and organizations and their own attendant methods, concerns, and critical conversations. "College English has lost its [unifying] referent," David B. Downing, Claude Mark Hurlbert, and Paula Mathieu (2002, 2) explain. The result, McComiskey (2006, 33) notes, is the feeling that "we cannot have meaningful conversations with our colleagues," let alone communicate the stakes of certain types of study to those outside a specialization's preferred discourse community. (I'll note that these professional conversations begin at the same time as, and tend to run parallel to, conversations about the nature of labor in English studies, a further indication of the close relationship of these relations.) The ruling relation of "confusion" compounded the development of a curriculum, at times catching the writing assignments and the design of the writing links in their crosshairs.

Parallel to the concerns of labor stratification in the gateway, questions about the nature of English studies were a powerful complex of confusions that organized the work of English 202 and English 197, especially how those faculty involved imagined the work of the writing links and the shared assignments. Here we begin to see why a study of the ways work took shape within the linked gateway is an important step for those concerned with writing and writing instruction: writing instruction and writing assignments were some of the primary sites in which these issues were hashed out. As one TA noted in our interview: "I'm really curious to see [and] to hear what the 202 instructors would say about this. Because it's sort of hard to know how to teach writing, even when you have these firm disciplinary parameters in mind. It's always a little difficult, but it doesn't have to be, really."

This response reveals the degree to which the story of crisis in English studies and the actualities of labor in the linked gateway took on force as a ruling relation and so coordinated much of the work of collaboration and shaped the way writing instruction took shape, even for individuals. Because the specialists in the department did not share vocabulary, a sense of key introductory concepts, or even values about what might be taught and how to teach it, the difficulties around identifying the conceptual and pedagogical centers of the class became a pressing topic of conversation for everyone involved in the gateway. These were not issues that could be ironed out in a single meeting, let alone a single course. These issues spoke to the problems of identity, consensus building, and purpose that have marked the national conversations of literary studies and regulated the scholarship of the discipline of English since the late 1980s. These issues not only informed but also stymied, challenged, and compelled the shapes writing assignments took.

IE requires that we recognize these ruling relations as series of undeniable influences on the shape work takes. What we see when we include the complicated array of ideals and identities indexed by the conditions identified in our study of shared writing assignments in the gateway, particularly "labor" and "disciplinary confusion," is that these powerful ruling relations worked in close tandem to produce an environment that centered the literature/large lecture faculty as experts (even if uncertain ones). These same relations de-centered others who worked for the linked gateway as proxies of that expertise. This social structuring of the gateway had an enormous influence on how work was carried out, determining process *and product*, often inseperably. The faculty who designed the large lecture held enormous influence over the development of most course schedules and related work practices, including the topic, critical approaches, and related sequencing of writing assignments. Consequently, the faculty instructors of linked courses assumed a near constant process of negotiation, development, and coordination of work processes—a time-consuming endeavor that left many of those involved in the gateway at odds with their own authority. IWP lecturers often referred to the linked gateway workflow as "unfolding in real time," a phrase that indicated the ways IWP faculty and TAs carried forth their work as a response to the ongoing negotiations of purpose, scope, and time line established by the lead faculty. Keeping the communicative channels open was an ongoing endeavor for all involved.

As I note above, all faculty in all courses are engaged in processes of negotiation within their classrooms as they bring their ideals of pedagogical practice and values around teaching into being. As individuals, we are always coordinating our work to align with what we understand as the principles and practices of a particular pedagogy. What the study of the gateway makes clear is that these sorts of materialities make a difference in how we do what we do; we are also always negotiating local values, histories, hierarchies, and established work processes. When we organize our work around pedagogical interventions and conceptions, we are engaged in the process of co-constituting a site of writing and writing instruction as one face of the institution.

HOW THE WORK OF WRITING ASSIGNMENTS TOOK SHAPE: LOGISTICS, NEGOTIATION, SLOW ALIGNMENT

> *I assumed that I, as an experienced graduate student, would find [teaching English 197] easy. Wrong! Instead, I was startled by how*

> *challenging it was to design good assignments based on texts I had not chosen and lectures whose content I could not entirely predict.*
>
> —TA 11 (IWP course file)

* * *

If this were a story of the labor of the field of writing studies or the ways faculty in English negotiated competing understandings of the "discipline" that is English studies, the story of the linked gateway's writing assignments might stop here. Instead, as a story of work within a collaborative but hierarchical curricular initiative, this study continued to inquire into multiple standpoints and ruling relations to understand the work processes of assignment design over the course of the collaboration. That is, even as IE starts with standpoint ("looking up" to uncover the experiences and practices of unique individuals), it also often inspires a broad understanding of the relationships that structure a site. The institutional ethnographer begins to develop a dialogic understanding of a site, a rich *and composite* vision.

The story of work that revealed itself as I looked up from the standpoints of those collaborating in the linked gateway came into visibility over time as I compiled narrative accounts across interviews, observations (of meetings and classes), email communications, and departmental documents concerning the courses. The documents and moments of confidence began to uncover how the ongoing work of the linked gateway evolved as the department and faculty collaborators reflected on how the courses took shape and discussed possible issues they had encountered. As a story of work and work processes, the story revealed demonstrates the ways knowing and active people negotiated the site of their work in alignment with the ruling relations, entrenched patterns of labor and expertise, and other expectations and understandings of the site.

It is important that we not read this story of work as an indictment of any one individual or any one department. As Campbell and Gregor (2002, 31) note, "People participate in social relations, often unknowingly, as they act competently and knowledgeably to concert and coordinate their own actions with professional standards." It is important to recognize that many faculty in the department were, at minimum, "knowing" and that many were also well-informed about these broader national politics. When asked, faculty expressed displeasure with the material conditions of higher education and the ways long-term disinvestment in higher ed had resulted in the foreclosure of support for TAs/graduate students and the humanities. Some were also vocal advocates for changing the ways these material conditions organized the particular labor conditions of TA and contingent work in the department.

No one involved in the gateway would have argued that the conditions for anyone were ideal, even as no one person had the means to change the conditions substantially. This difficult reality is one of the other primary outcomes of the study of institutional sites of writing—we often come to realize (over and again, at times) that even empowered and aware individuals must work within the co-constituted contexts of their sites. Moments of resistance and divergence, even when significant in the slow processes of long-term change, are often invisible to all but a small handful of people. Moments of open and visible resistance may have no long-lasting impact at all. Sometimes institutional change is far harder to achieve than we would like.

IE's framework for understanding our work reminds us as well that the collaborative nature of the gateway positioned each of the faculty—literature, lead IWP, and TA—in ways that seemed to make "natural sense" within the logic of the department and the linked gateway itself. And quarter by quarter, with opportunities for faculty to reflect on what was working and what was not, the process of developing shared assignments for the linked gateway did adapt to the multiple concerns of those involved. The process regularized and congealed around the authority of the literature faculty but was also far more equitable over time for the lead IWP faculty. This is how ruling relations impact the shape of work: across the time and space of the collaboration, people work within their roles, dynamically evolving and aligning what they do as they are informed by their interactions with others. Practice, experience, labor, and expertise are always uneven, flexible (to some degree), and changeable influences—ebbing, flowing, and influencing one another below the overt institutional discourses that most coordinate shared efforts. In the linked gateway, faculty took on these roles in ways that sustained the collaboration, building relationships over time and focusing on issues they could solve within the structural order of the site. They problem-solved in ways that made sense within the moment and the larger context of departmental culture.

For clarity and to again demonstrate how IE brings the construction of work to light, I trace the work of literature faculty, lead IWP faculty, and TAs separately.

Literature Faculty Work

In the earliest iterations of the linked gateway, the readings, assignments, critical approaches, and schedule for major writing projects were generated almost exclusively by the lead faculty in charge of the lecture. But here we see a difference in how work and its processes took shape for lead faculty versus others in the linked gateway—differences that return us to the undeniable materialities of all work: the ruling relations of the linked gateway did not require the same degree of adaptability from the literature faculty who taught the lecture as they did from others who were required to build their courses and writing assignments in relation to the lecture. In meetings and through the emails they sent, literature faculty assumed a role of disciplinary expert. The literature faculty primarily explained how they had come to develop the content of the lecture (the readings, assignments, and critical structure) and what they found valuable in these particular choices, fostering an awareness of how their choices reflected trends and attitudes in the discipline at large. Though there was always variation among individuals, the work of literature faculty was, then, often most influenced by their relationships with the department and the discipline.

IWP Faculty Work

As a result of their role as representatives of the IWP, the lead IWP faculty concerned themselves with the logistics between the lecture and the links. The IWP faculty wrote the assignments, mindful that this work was a negotiation of their relationship with the literature faculty (so honoring the goals and structures important to those faculty) and offering attention to the logistical needs of the TAs. This positioned them as the coaches of TAs and arbiters of many difficulties; when TAs struggled to understand an assignment or an aspect of the large lecture, the IWP faculty were on the first line, talking through and breaking down the ideas of the lecture, reading, or assignment for TAs. Increasingly, in later iterations of the linked gateway, the lead IWP lecturer was invited by the literature faculty leading the lecture to offer feedback on the reading lists and critical approaches in the lecture, to lead or heavily assist with the writing assignments, and to have more input into the schedule for assignments. That is, as the quarters progressed, the role of the lead IWP faculty expanded tremendously. (And indeed, most literature faculty were generously and authentically engaged in the later collaborations.)

Over time, then, the work of the IWP faculty began to adapt a more openly mediative stance and to take on more authority than in early versions of the collaboration. The IWP faculty often delivered the schedule and assignments to TAs with a brief rationale and an example handout about the expectations for student writers, such as the ways writers might make a "claim" in the essay they would write, how to conduct research to support the close reading of a poem, and how to integrate quotations. The IWP faculty also circulated handouts and course activities in support of the IWP's preferred pedagogical approaches, such as student-faculty conferencing, the value of peer review, how students might respond to faculty feedback, and how to encourage student use of the writing center. These activities served as reminders of expectations for TA practice in the courses but did not prescribe those practices or the exact shapes they took. The assignments and approaches developed by the IWP faculty (with the literature faculty's input or approval) were often discussed in meetings in which the writing link instructors shared additional resources, developed their ideas about how they would work with the writing assignments they had been given, and, when necessary, raised questions. Though there was always variation among individuals, the work of the lead IWP faculty was most often influenced by their relationships to the literature faculty who designed the lecture and their willingness and abilities to act as coaches and guides to TAs.

TA Work

Because of their responsibility for the writing links, TA work was often conceptualized in relationship to student writing and writers. In their work with student writers, TAs tended to take up where the large lecture left off, adopting the writing assignments others had developed. In their courses and in meetings, they often focused on reviewing aspects of the lecture (such as close reading practice) as a means to gain authority over the writing assignments, as a performative means to appropriate the discourse that had been presented in the large lecture, and to become more clear about how they would authorize the evaluation of student writing.

TAs were often mindful of their own roles within their courses, focusing much of their teaching on writing as an English major (in a generalized way) as a means to both integrate the critical frames the lecture entailed (especially if those frames were new to them) and arbitrate the ideals of writing for undergraduates new to the major. As such, many took on postures in their courses that allowed them to move among playing insider guide to the major or discipline, close reading and writing coach, and finally evaluator or arbiter of student responses. Work with IE helps us understand that these roles were taken on as a means to negotiate the writing assignments produced by others and so were always inflected by the information offered and moments of expertise performed by other players in the gateway. As such, these moves often assumed an overtly relational tenor.

TAs were not overtly discouraged from developing their own materials in the writing links per se. But as the semesters of the linked gateway continued and the lecture and writing links began to be more tightly coordinated, the culture of the linked gateway tended to dissuade too much deviation from shared resources and assignments. Ironically, as the expectations for closer collaboration increased (a means to ameliorate concerns over labor and questions about how the lecture took its focus), uncertainties around who had the authority to write, rewrite, and "teach off book" also increased.

Some TAs appreciated the closer collaborations and the restrictions they entailed. As one wrote in her course file:

> Each quarter the communication between the 197 TAs and the lecturer improved, and each quarter the writing sections coordinated more closely with one another. The more we stressed teamwork, the happier my students seemed. This quarter the issue of coordination between [*sic*] the three modes of instruction did not even come up . . . Though the writing sections have much less autonomy than they had a year ago, the result of the close team approach definitely appears to be worth that price. (TA 15 [IWP course file])

But there is another important note about the shape of work and work processes for TAs here as well. Overwhelmingly, when asked about their work and the work processes of the gateway, many other TAs expressed a sense of disenfranchisement from the writing assignments they were given. As a result, their discussions of their work tended to muddy logistical concerns (how they were enabled to teach) with other, more overtly pedagogical aspects of their teaching (how they might support student learning). Witnessing these moments of negotiation was revealing—these conversations revealed that within the contexts of the gateway, pedagogy was more *material process* than orienting concept. And despite the dramatic attempts to find, design, or impose a shared pedagogy, in the end pedagogy always took shape as a highly individualized set of choices. I discuss this finding and the ways it pushed on ideals of pedagogy active in our field in the conclusion of this chapter.

Consider the following interview responses and accounts of teaching from the IWP's TA course files:

> **TA 10 (IWP course file):** Often we (the 197 instructors) were encouraged to hand out essay prompts at the beginning of each new writing cycle.

Doing so I found that my essay prompts were largely unsatisfactory and not sufficiently focused when it came time for the students to write their first drafts.

* * *

TA 7 (personal interview): There have been times where the assignments have been . . . so out of sync . . . that it's really clear that there hasn't been a good recognition of the kind of cycles that we have to work with in 197 and how those could be worked into the lecture . . . And the students definitely always comment on it when the classes seem out of sync and they're not really sure what the relationship is between the two classes.

It is clear from the above responses that TAs felt a number of pressing concerns in relation to the work of English 197. Keeping up with new content in the large lecture, adapting their own course schedules to accommodate changes in the lecture, understanding assignments they would administer, and trying to establish a pedagogical relationship between the lecture and links greatly occupied the energies of TAs. The closer collaborations did not seem to ameliorate these concerns.

The hints of resistance that flourished within this narrative of labor, uncertain pedagogy, and hierarchy are intriguing—clearly, TA resistance bears a role in the development of assignments as well. One of the many complicating factors here is how the linked gateway did and did not position TAs as "expertise insiders" (Rankin and Campbell. 2009, n.p.)—clearly, being distanced from the process of creating writing assignments influenced the ways TAs aligned their own practices in the larger project of the gateway. Sadly, the majority of TAs did not speak freely about what they may have been doing "off book," and so this portion of the story must remain untold. There are likely many reasons for this silence. Because many TAs were in the last stages of departmental funding, they often chose not to share what they were doing in courses as a means of staying clear of unwanted scrutiny or the threat of non-renewal. (I refer readers back to the response of one TA to my request for an interview: she declined because she did not want to "bite the hand that feeds me.")

Yet even these responses are not the full story of how writing assignments in 202 and 197 took shape. Many TAs, like the one quoted above, assumed an overt posture of negotiation and acquiescence to manage their work. Consider the following descriptions of teaching strategies shared with the IWP leadership in TA course files:

TA 11 (IWP course file): By far the most challenging aspect of [teaching English 197 and] designing essay prompts was trying to strike an appropriate balance between the need to conform to cooperative goals and strategies and the desire to be creative and proactive in the classroom. So that students didn't feel unfairly treated, it was vital to have some consistency across the 197 sections. At the same time, without some degree of autonomy, it is difficult to teach well and to feel accountable for what transpires in the classroom. I struggled all quarter to strike that ideal balance, and the struggle is reflected in my paper assignments.

* * *

TA 9 (IWP course file): My work with English 197/English 202 certainly has been an experience in learning how to manage and negotiate the various demands and goals of the English department, the IWP, and my own teaching objectives.

* * *

In some ways, it is difficult not to read the politeness of these responses as a gentle means of speaking truth to power. "Thank you for the opportunity to teach this course," another TA wrote, moving as other TAs did as well to indirectly reference the benefits teaching for the gateway offered, particularly the meager stipend and tuition waiver. This stance of negotiation, then, was closely related to the very means by which TAs sustained themselves and was closely linked to their own investments in their ongoing work on a PhD in a beleaguered and underfunded field.

Observations of the linked gateway's many meetings, communications, and course sessions revealed that logistics remained an ever pressing concern, particularly for those who taught the writing links. Many of the strategies adopted were an effort to help TAs save time, find a more comfortable relationship within the linked gateway, and smooth ongoing relations between those who were positioned differently within the collaborative endeavor. Despite the good intentions of all involved, the difficulties of organizing the linked gateway's writing assignments persisted. Conversations about the topic, critical approach, and scope of assignments—if not the scaffolding and schedule of the lecture—often consumed meetings and dominated many emails. But as a local face of national issues—national trends in higher education labor, national issues in finding a center for English studies, national issues in understanding how student writing support and well-integrated writing instruction fits into the larger missions of university education—these issues remained largely unsettled in the gateway. No one was entirely empowered to make the changes necessary to smooth the way substantially.

The writing assignments developed for the writing links sat at the conjunction of these material concerns—the assignments and attendant critical frames needed to be clear to all involved, extending and deepening the work of the lecture while remaining accessible to the TAs who would take them into their isolated classrooms to work with students. The assignments needed to be appropriately sequenced to reflect the ways TAs expected a writing course to unfold. The assignments needed to follow a schedule (with some flexibility) so that all writing link instructors could run their own courses more manageably as well. Over time and to different degrees, the writing assignments increasingly reflected these multiple points of negotiation, even as they remained focused on carrying out the main learning goal identified by the literature faculty leading the lecture.

More important, over time, as logistics and confusion over possible pedagogical approaches remained pressing, many TAs talked back to the lead faculty and IWP mentors as they were able—sharing their concerns, asking questions, and posing new approaches to the work of their classes. IWP faculty used the feedback from TAs to talk back persuasively to the lead faculty and department as they were able, discussing the difficulties of class management, communication, and clarity in expectations. The lead faculty and the department listened with the institutional circuits that were enabled, adapted their stances slightly, and offered new processes to ameliorate some of the issues TAs faced. Slowly, quarter by quarter, the work of the linked gateway evolved—time lines became more workable for TAs and the lecture course more amenable to thinking about the shape of teaching writing as a starting point for the development of the lectures' readings and activities. As one IWP faculty member noted:

> We've tried really hard to tap across the divide that is writing instruction and the discipline . . . I think there's been lots of close and productive discussion . . . I don't know if the courses can be integrated enough, though I would characterize them as increasingly integrated.

And as a senior literature faculty shared with me:

> I actually feel like I have an understanding of what they do in IWP and in the writing link now. But to be perfectly honest, I had a pretty sketchy sense going in. It's actually, I think, one of the problems with the course—I mean, that's not a news flash. I think that's actually a kind of institutional, structural question—one doesn't exactly—I believe the IWP faculty are our colleagues, but we don't, faculty on the lit and cultural side don't have much connection to them unless we teach this course.

The official writing assignments of the linked gateway began to take shape as a manifestation of this process of listening and more intentional collaboration. TAs did continue to revise assignments and often did so "off book," sometimes as a process of making sense of these learning tools and sometimes as a process of reclaiming the authority they felt they lost in the collaboration. That said, all efforts across the board continued to align within the prevailing logics of the linked gateway. As no one was empowered or incentivized to change the larger structures of employment, many of the issues of standpoint and ruling relations simply did not change in any substantive way. The holistic process of IE required that I continue to look into the evolution of work over time, compiling this story to recognize multiple perspectives even as I remained fairly concerned for the ways the linked gateway positioned the work of TAs.

Here I provide a brief coda of sorts: eleven years after the initial study, I corresponded with some of the faculty I worked closely with about the linked gateway and its ongoing evolution. My sources suggested that individuals involved with the courses continue, even these many years after the initial development of the class, to negotiate the same difficulties of organization I discuss here. The department has attempted to alter the dynamic of the course with several different arrangements of labor: bringing in TAs at the earlier stages of their PhD study; providing more, longer, and specific training before the quarter begins; and mentoring those TAs more closely around writing instruction through the course of the semester. The department has also renumbered the courses so that undergraduates take them later in their work in the major. My correspondents suggest that no one is entirely satisfied despite these efforts, the devotion of significant resources, and the pervasive concern that undergraduates benefit from courses that prepare them to understand the written work of the English major.

At the time of this writing, the course is no longer required for all undergraduate English majors, and the department is considering dropping the writing link entirely because of the expense of IWP and TA labor.

WHEN THE MATERIALITIES OF OUR WORK SPEAK

> *You know, we go to a department meeting and people start complaining about the fact that our graduating students in our senior seminars can't write for beans. And so, that's why we invented this gateway, in a sense, because the people who were taking senior seminars, we weren't sure they were as capable as they should be to write—even sensibly—critical writing as opposed to persuasive essays.*
>
> —Director, English undergraduate education

This story of work and work processes in the linked gateway reveals an important reality that is often overlooked in conversations about pedagogy in writing studies. We often speak of pedagogical practice as if what people do takes place in an untethered, even universal, time and space. Moreover, despite our frequent use of the term *pedagogy*, we have rarely attempted to define it or to map the many ways its common use opens out in our field's discursive practices. Amy Rupiper Taggart, H. Brooke Hessler, and Kurt Schick (2014, 2, original emphasis) recognize this gap as they argue that "[many] of us come to understand the term *pedagogy* inductively" based on our own experiences as students and in coursework. The field of composition, these authors argue, has defined the term *indirectly*, focusing extensively on "building systems for classifying and contrasting pedagogical approaches" (2) while overlooking the need for a broader theoretical grounding. Even historically important works in the field—for example, James A. Berlin's "Contemporary Composition: The Major Pedagogical Theories" (1982, 766), which notes that pedagogy is a "version of reality" that orients teachers, researchers, and scholars—follow the primary scholarly move of differentiating one pedagogical approach from one another. Taggart, Hessler, and Schick step into this gap to posit pedagogy as an "umbrella term" with theoretical, research-based, rhetorical, and personal faces. They then define pedagogy to draw on each of these domains: "Composition pedagogy is a body of knowledge consisting of theories of and research on teaching, learning, writing, and rhetoric and the related practice that emerges. It is a deliberate integration of theory research, personal philosophy, and rhetorical praxis into composition instruction at all levels from the daily lesson plan to the writing program and the communities it serves" (2014, 3). Using IE to review the work of a writing assignment uncovers a different story of pedagogy, one that challenges each of these discreet centers to the umbrella term as Taggart, Hessler, and Schick define it.

Pedagogy in the linked gateway was not at all a free-standing entity that oriented the teaching of others in a neutral or conceptual sense. In fact, pedagogy in the linked gateway was rarely theoretical or rhetorical and even more rarely research-based. Because of the collaborative nature of the linked gateway, pedagogy was not necessarily personal either—though those working for the shared initiative often did make unique choices within the overall endeavor. Study of the linked gateway extends these idealized centers of our definitions of pedagogy (and the initiatives, practices, and moments of interaction coordinated by particular pedagogical conceptions), demonstrating that pedagogy is also a set of material conditions and processes of negotiation. In fact, what we call pedagogy may be more effectively thought of as a highly situated process of negotiation, generated in the moments where a number of social forces bump against and even abrade one another as the tools of writing instruction take shape. Our field may conceive of pedagogy as a theoretical, rhetorical, research-based, and personal ideal, but the reality is that pedagogy in a local sense takes shape in each and every collaborative discussion about linked courses, takes shape again in private discussions between collaborators, and takes a new face again in the writing assignments designed and redesigned in the gateway. As one of the primary influences on our work, pedagogy can be understood as a site that actively co-constitutes our institutions.

IE offers an important but missing granular, material, and locally grounded understanding of the big ideals of our field, revealing that our concepts are in fact also processes, which invent and reinvent themselves within highly situated, local, and material contexts. When informed by the IE framework, the story a writing assignment tells is a story of the particularities of work and its many subtending processes. The uncovering of experience and practice in the UW English department's linked-course initiative—a process of looking up from the standpoints of the many different collaborators—allows us to see how the ideals of pedagogy do and do not take face as they are regenerated with the specific material contexts of a site. *We see that pedagogy in a local sense is highly individualized and situated.*

This study's findings subsequently push on the ideals of writing studies and WAC/WID work, which often presume a unified understanding of disciplinary ways of doing, knowing, and being as the center of pedagogical models. When we use a methodology that systematically foregrounds the unique material relations of our work as writing instructors, our research activities better demonstrate the ways our concepts are always co-constituted in the moment and in the particular—generated in the moment that knowing individuals negotiate material relations, expertise, identity, and personal investments. We come to understand the relations that constitute our actual work as members of a research-driven field.

3

THE ANNUAL REVIEW AS "BOSS TEXT" AND THE COORDINATION OF WRITING CENTER WORK

Uncovering Disjunctions between Local and National Discourse

> *My advice to every WC director: keep one pair of dress shoes and one pair of Chucks in your office . . . 'Cause either you're running like the devil (Chucks) or you're meeting with a dean (dress).*
>
> —Staff and Faculty Standpoints Project First-Year Writing Faculty 2 (email exchange)

> *When we are teaching writing, when we are really teaching anything, when we are working with students, and when we are working within a learning environment, we cannot ignore that we are in a web, we are in a social context. We cannot ignore that the people we are working with bring their own ideas and bring their own understandings of the work we are doing to this. We are negotiating and navigating together constantly. I learn this lesson daily. It has been a part of my work in writing centers from day one.*
>
> —Faculty and Staff Standpoints Project Participant 4 (personal interview)

Since the late 1980s, writing center professionals have been gravely concerned about the status and structure of writing center work. National email listserv memberships regularly take up the interconnectedness of institutional rank, disciplinary identity, and the standing of writing centers. Those involved worry over the rhetorical impact of titles for the leaders of writing centers. (Liaison? Coordinator? Director? Writing program administrator? [see Healy 1995; M. Harris 1990, 2002].) They discuss the ideal shape of writing center administrator positions. (Staff or faculty? [see Elliot 1990].) They discuss the difficulties many administrators have faced when explaining the range of their activities to department chairs, deans, and other administrators on campus. (Does the work of the center count as service, or is it evaluated some other way?

DOI: 10.7330/9781607328674.c003

How is it evaluated during the tenure process? [see Olson and Ashton-Jones 1988; Murphy and Stay 2012].)

Scholarly voices argue in-kind. Melissa Ianetta and her colleagues (2006), for instance, trace conversations in the field to reveal a common "spectrum" of imagined and recurrent standpoints. Persistent trends in these conversations reveal thorny "questions of credentialing, working conditions, and professional authority" in relation to conceptions of the work writing center professionals carry out (Ianetta et al. 2006, 11). Meanwhile, Neal Lerner (2000) has argued that the material and intellectual conditions of some campuses will chronically limit the opportunities available to writing center professionals within those local contexts. Some writing center professionals will be "haves" and others "have nots," with the local conditions of campuses significantly impacting the type of work that can be carried out (Lerner 2000, 10). The "troubling and foreboding" nature of these conversations in the field's literature and lore, as Anne Ellen Geller and Harry Denny (2013, 99) have acknowledged, brings to light continuing "struggles over intellectual labor and disciplinary identity at the nexus of writing centers, writing program administration, composition scholarship, and English studies."

Although these conversations have been faithful to a central professional worry, Nicole Caswell, Jackie Grutsch McKinney, and Rebecca Jackson observe that much of the field's published research on writing center labor has tended to focus on the "typical" nature of programs and positions. They note that there has been little sustained or systematic effort to study the situated experiences of writing center administrators within the grounded actualities of their work lives. Caswell, McKinney, and Jackson (2016, 10) argue that without focused attention to the "particular contours and complexities of different institutional contexts," professionals in writing center studies will miss out on "facets of writing center administrator labor that other types of research or scholarship have up to now left invisible." They call for further attention to the processes and conditions that organize and coordinate the actual work of writing center professionals within their local settings.

I note a similar dynamic in chapters 1 and 2: researchers in writing studies (writing center professionals among them) have often taken up critiques of the construction of our work and its value in writing programs and classrooms, but we have tended to do so in ways that are removed from the actual institutional contexts of that work. Without close attention to how work takes shape within local settings, we may easily misunderstand what actual people do within sites of writing. A close analysis of how professionals—writing center administrators, writing program administrators, faculty, students—actually negotiate the specific discourses of their institutions in alignment (or not) with the discourses of the field is one means by which institutional ethnographers might bring to light the actualities of experience and practice that are the institution in action. As we turn our attention to what individuals actually do, we are able to trace the factors and forces that influence them as they carry out their everyday work.

In this chapter I explore the situated nature of our work through a study of the influence of the HR designation and the annual review process on staff and faculty work lives. The study begins with a general inquiry into how the HR designation organizes the work of writing center administrators, then moves to follow the annual review process of six writing center professionals who hold faculty and staff positions at different types of institutions. These employment designations and employment review texts act as "boss texts," a term coined by Dorothy Smith (Griffith and Smith 2014, 12) to acknowledge that some texts exert a powerful material and local influence over the everyday work lives of professionals. All texts, in the IE framework, have an "architectural significance," replicating ideals of practice in order to coordinate what people do across time and space. "Boss texts" accrue a particular type of authority within local settings, as they circulate ideals of accountability, professionalism, and disciplinarity. "Boss texts" set the conditions on which "an institutional course of action can follow" (Griffith and Smith 2014, 12), seeking to regulate and standardize experience and practice as well as mediate the idiosyncrasies and variability of local settings.

Seeking to understand the work of these boss texts and to explore the material actualities they coordinate, this project collected survey data, conducted multiple interviews about the nature of these professionals' work lives (including the processes of their annual and third-year reviews), and analyzed the language of annual and third-year review documents. The findings of this study reveal that many writing center administrators often struggle to make manifest the values of the field in light of local discourses, pedagogical cultures, and expectations. Even in positions that are ostensibly set up to reflect the value systems central to writing center studies, the institutional mechanisms that coordinate and review the local work of administrators often refuse or resist alignment with the field's values, catching writing center professionals between the ideals of their work as conceived by discussions in the field and the realities of their work in local settings.

When we consider the relationships among boss texts, the ruling relations that order the field of writing studies, and the standpoints writing center professionals adopt within local contexts, clear disjunctions emerge between national and local conversations about writing center work. Systematic study into how our work is coordinated by these texts, how boss texts enact processes of evaluation and classification, and the means by which these texts organize the work actually carried out by writing center professionals can tell us new stories about the questions of professional status and identity that remain central to disciplinary communities of writing studies. Informed by these new stories, we might note the degree to which our national conversations have and have not made a difference in the shape of writing center work within local contexts. We are then able to understand the processes that continue to organize that work locally and nationally.

HR DOCUMENTS AS BOSS TEXTS: THE SYSTEMATIC STUDY OF ACTUALITIES

> *[People] enact the world they inhabit and know about, in concert with other people and, of course, with the technologies that people operate.*
>
> —Marie Campbell and Frances Gregor, *Mapping Social Relations: A Primer in Doing Institutional Ethnography*

> *We wondered about the impact of HR classification or its related discursive child, a job description, on how work gets done in the field. We began to think a good deal about how individuals come into their institutional work with significantly different expectations about what their work will entail. These points of origination make a difference to what gets done, how it gets done, by whom, and for what purposes.*
>
> —LaFrance and Nicolas, "Institutional Ethnography as Materialist Framework for Writing Program Research and the Faculty-Staff Work Standpoints Project"

I have written elsewhere with Melissa Nicolas about the power of the HR designation (and related employment documents and practices) to organize our everyday work lives. For many employees, HR designation "sometimes equates to place within a work site hierarchy [as it] cues us to specific concerns for the larger social context that surrounds universities and writing programs" (LaFrance and Nicolas 2012, 137). Organizational texts, such as the annual review, position descriptions, advertisements for employment opportunities, and contracts, have an undeniable architectural significance in our work lives, shaping what we do and how we do it. These records grant access and afford privilege, aligning our work in particular ways with specific visions of institutional mission. Close research-driven attention to the representations and valences assigned by employment texts has the possibility of uncovering new understandings about how our work is coordinated within the social hierarchies, modes of authorities, and specific value systems of our local sites. These efforts reveal what happens when our field's national constructions of work play out in the situated contexts of the sites of writing we study.

Like the change of perspective that comes with rethinking institutions as sites that are co-constituted in the moments when knowing individuals take up practice toward some ends, recognizing the role texts play in shaping the actual work of people is a crucial piece of coming to understand and study how things happen within institutional sites of writing. "Recognizing how people's work is controlled, managed, and, more generally, coordinated through the medium of texts of many kinds is integral to the very possibility of taking ethnography beyond what can be learned from local observation while keeping it anchored in the local setting of people's work," Smith writes (Griffith and Smith 2014, 340). All texts carry ruling relations across settings and to different people. Institutional texts also "nominalize" and "objectify" knowledges, creating an over-determined sense of what goes on in a location—a conceptual process that erases divergences, disjunctions, and differences of experience and practice.

The result, according to the Society for the Study of Social Problems (2006, 293), is that "frequently, and in systematic ways, the categories and conceptual frameworks of administration are inattentive to the actual circumstances of the diverse lives people live in contemporary societies. Frequently, and systematically, the slippages between everyday lives and objectified knowledge of those lives operate to produce and perpetuate circumstances that constitute social problems." That is, as employment texts organize our work, they often do so in ways that reflect institutional norms, values, and practices—a process that can come into conflict with the norms, values, and practices that are central to disciplinary or professional identity.

The annual review (and its related textually mediated practices) is a transactional practice that grounds our ongoing conversations about the status and value of our work in the actualities of the everyday doing, knowing, and being of real people. As a "boss text," in Smith's lexicon, the annual review is a particularly powerful institutional apparatus that "governs" the coordination of work, anchoring conceptions of that work in generalized categories of labor that have taken shape in local settings. Laura Bisaillon (2012, 610) defines the "boss" or "governing" text as

> a text or set of texts that supplies the context for what we can see, hear, and know. There are subsidiary documents that come into being and are organized under these texts, which are positioned at the top of a hierarchy of texts. Dorothy Smith (2010) explains that boss texts are authorized through institutional procedures through which specific people are instructed to carry out specific practices. Boss texts coordinate organizational relations so "how people work is controlled in conformity with the selective requirements of the boss text . . . There are layers and layers of them" (D. Smith, 2010, not published, on file with author).

As a text that governs practice, the annual review requires an employee to negotiate the institutional values that prescribe the employee's position, describing and evaluating the practices that constitute his or her work in relation to the institution's understanding of the shape, quality, and value of that work. Encoding a broad possible array of institutional values and understandings, the annual review process may lend an institutional visibility and recognizable value to—or erase, minimize, and diminish—the work writing center administrators carry out. This on-the-ground recognition of the language and practices of the annual employment review has been a missing part of the stories circulated in the field about professional work in writing centers.

BACKGROUND: THE STAFF AND FACULTY STANDPOINTS PROJECT

This chapter draws on the Staff and Faculty Standpoints project, a multi-institutional project I developed in collaboration with Melissa Nicolas. We set out to uncover the differences in everyday work for faculty and staff writing center administrators. Specifically, we sought to understand how HR designations like "staff" or "faculty" make a difference in everyday work practice for people who serve in similar positions that are ranked differently by their institutional hierarchies. While we knew it was not always true that staff members lacked the same opportunities and challenges as faculty, we had noticed prevalent assumptions in higher education that, as Paula M. Krebs (2003, B5) has noted, these positions mirrored the class-based distinction between upstairs and downstairs in the Victorian era. Anecdotally, we felt that our field tended to generalize about the work we all carried out, unintentionally ignoring significant differences in the ways our work was constructed, carried out, and understood by discussions in the scholarship of the field.

Melissa and I wondered how the differences between staff and faculty writing center administrators might play out in the actual everyday contexts of different centers. What conversations and recognitions might be missing from the writing center scholarship? What we found in the course of our initial study was that local contexts are often more complex than our national professional conversations about the status of writing center work tended to acknowledge. The work we piloted in the Staff and Faculty Standpoints project lent important background to my continuing study of the annual review process. I combine the results of the pilot and annual review study here because the two projects inform one another nicely.

The interplay between individual standpoint and the boss text is an important element of analysis for this work. As I note in chapter 1, standpoint is a concept that aids the institutional ethnographer in uncovering the experiences and practices of "an anchor group" (DeVault 2008, 5). As a central analytic for the work of the institutional ethnographer, standpoint foregrounds the ways individuals are unique and therefore uniquely experience the broad social relations and institutional circuits (such as those organized by boss texts) in which they are embedded. Standpoint recognizes that how people negotiate their social circumstances as professionals is entirely wrapped up in their ways of being in the world—who we are, what we know, how we are seen by others, our designated roles, and how we have been credentialed or come by our experiences all play a role in how we carry out our daily work. A focus on standpoint allows the institutional ethnographer to trace the interplay between the ruling relations and material conditions that surround and inform an individual's work within an institution.

As boss texts, HR designations and their attendant annual review processes encode a series of procedures, values, and institutional conditions that demand negotiation. Literally a notation on a piece of paper or electronic record, these categories of employment sanction generalized classifications of status, task, and value for otherwise discrete positions within and across institutions. An analysis of HR designation in writing center communities, I believed, could help us to make visible the situated variability of experience, reward, and recognition attached to these positions—allowing us to explore how the shape of work practices for one employee could be dramatically different from the practices of another employee as a result of numerous personal, institutional, and cultural factors that arise out of the categorization of their work within a hierarchical system of labor. Our initial results suggested that further analysis of the annual review processes might help us come to a deeper understanding of how the work of writing center administrators is institutionally shaped toward specific ends.

Indeed, the actual expectations for a staff member overseeing a writing program or writing center may be no different in some locations than for a faculty member running the very same program at a different institution—but in many institutions, the work of each would be *granted different values.* In many locations, these notions of value correlate with the distribution of resources, such as merit pay increases, office space, access to technology, professional development opportunities, travel funding, or others. We also note the particular power of HR documents to dramatically mediate our professional lives, producing often well-scripted relationships with and within the institution in their foundational generalizations.

As I note above, performance review processes are institutional mechanisms that exert an undeniable discursive force in the day-to-day lives of employees. These documents may articulate us to enabling or limiting job descriptions or contractually outline the expectations for our daily and long-term practices. These documents determine when our work year and day begins and ends, the size of our standard teaching loads, what constitutes an effectively active research agenda, guidelines for tenure and promotion, and other elements of our work. A simple distinction between staff and faculty can make an enormous difference in the conceptions of an individual's workday, work life, and professional standing. A document such as a time card, a job description, or a performance review can be said to order (and discursively represent) our institutional experiences in key ways. These texts are so rolled up in the nature of our institutions that it is easy to take the work they do for granted, overlooking their significance in the ways they coordinate our work with the work of others.

To begin to understand the role HR designation plays in the everyday lives of writing center administrators, we initially collected general information about the daily work lives of administrators through a large national survey (posted on the national writing center email listserv). This initial work uncovered a series of general trends in the everyday work of respondents that enabled us to think more about how HR designation coordinates the daily activities of writing center administrators—an informed background that provides provocative groundwork for a more thorough ethnographic analysis of writing center annual review processes.

What I have learned as I continued this project, moving from an initial general interest in the coordinating force of the HR designation to the more focused concern for the power of the annual performance review, is that *on a macro-level the patterns of the everyday work of writing center administrators correlate closely with HR designation. The annual review is the apparatus that carries out, and at times intensifies, the coordinating power of the HR designation, assigning value to the work carried out.* Writing center administrators have very real and ongoing concerns for the recognition of their labor and the continuing low status that attends the work of the writing center—in many ways, these concerns are borne out as we uncover the experiences of administrators undergoing their reviews. Especially as we look at the differences in the processes of performance review for faculty versus staff administrators, we can see that institutions value the labor of these individuals in dramatically different ways. Staff are evaluated quite differently from faculty, and both staff and faculty writing center administrators at times struggle to negotiate the review systems that are designed for their peers. This project reveals that a number of confusions remain about the nature of and expertise attached to the work of the writing center. These overall confusions have a role in shaping the daily experiences of these administrators within the centers they lead—a reality much commented upon in the literature of the field (see, for instance, Lerner 2000; Smoot 1985; Perdue 1991).

INITIAL SURVEY DATA COLLECTION: UNCOVERING CRITICAL STANDPOINTS

Attempting to account for the various ways HR designation constructs writing center work in local settings seemed no simple task when we began this project; any writing center is likely to have a variety of positions, from undergraduate tutors to graduate tutors, to staff who do administrative work, to the professionals who direct the work of all involved. Larger centers may have one or two levels of administrative leadership as well as assistant administrators, administrators, and faculty liaisons. To complicate matters on the national level, some campuses have no tenure-line faculty involved in their writing centers, while in others the only "permanent" position is a tenured faculty member. Some centers have paid professional tutors who teach, and others have volunteer tutors. Because of the difficulty in accounting for the full range of positions and because the field of writing studies has for so long been concerned with the status of the administrator of all sorts of writing programs, our study focused on the differences we could uncover between administrators who were classified as staff and those classified as faculty. (We allowed participants to determine for themselves which of these categories they fit.)

Table 3.1. Respondent demographics

Position Held*	42 full-time staff
	74 full-time faculty
	25 non-tenure track
	49 tenure track
	7 "adjunct" faculty
Gender	92 female (59%)
	36 male (23%)
	26 did not identify (19%)
Age	4 ages 18 to 24 (3%)
	19 ages 25 to 34 (12%)
	47 ages 35 to 50 (30%)
	44 ages 51 to 65 (29%)
	8 ages 66 to 100 (5%)
	32 skipped (21%)
Degree Held	13 BAs (8%)
	36 MAs (23%)
	56 PhDs (36%)
	49 skipped (31%)

* Not all respondents answered this question.

As Melissa and I describe, we composed a twenty-nine–question online survey that focused on how the work of a writing center administrator was constructed around the HR designation. We recruited participants through the national writing center email list (WCenter-L). A total of 154 responses rolled in during the summer and early fall of 2010. The basic demographics indicated by survey respondents (table 3.1) are revealing in and of themselves. The majority of our respondents indicated that they hold "faculty" positions (74 of 154), and the majority of survey respondents noted that they were female (59%), which lends legitimacy to ongoing concerns in writing center circles about the gendering or feminization of writing centers. More people with PhDs responded than did those with BAs or MAs. Overwhelmingly, respondents indicated that they were between the ages of 25 and 65.

As we cross-referenced responses to our questions about demographics, we began to see some familiar correspondences between the institutional rank of the administrators we surveyed and the highest degree held. Table 3.2 indicates a high and likely unsurprising correlation

Table 3.2. Highest degree held

	Staff n = 42	*Non-TT n = 25*	*TT n = 49*
Bachelor's	31%	0%	0%
Master's	64.3%	45.8%	16.3%
Doctorate	4.8%	54.2%	83.7%

between holding a PhD and holding a tenure-line faculty position, for instance. Respondents with PhDs also indicated having TT and non-TT faculty lines as well, though to a lesser degree. Those with MAs were most likely to hold staff positions, and BA respondents indicated primarily holding staff positions. This is where our initial survey data collection began to reveal different aspects of work life organization around HR designation.

But when we asked "on average, how many hours a week do you work?" we began to see other differences in everyday work appear in responses (table 3.3). Those who identified themselves as holding faculty positions primarily work over forty hours a week. Those who identified as staff respondents primarily stay within forty hours weekly. The qualitative responses of faculty participants describe the work week as open-ended, noting that they work nights, weekends, and holidays on top of the typically 9-to-5 workday. Staff respondents described their working week as finite, with clear beginnings and endings, breaks, and fewer mentions of working on weekends. These responses are revealing of the ways HR designations shape the work lives of people in comparable positions in rather different ways.

Further differences around the HR designation emerged in response to our question "how many hours of your work week do you spend in the actual writing center" (table 3.4). Respondents indicated that 45 percent of staff spent all of their work week in the center, but only 16.7 percent of non-TT faculty and only 2.1 percent of TT faculty indicated that they did so. These findings seemed to reveal significant differences in how work was actually organized around HR designation. According to our survey participants, the work life of the staff administrator is spent in the center. "I'm expected to be in the center from 9 to 6 each day," a participant with a staff position told me in our interview. "I post my hours. I'm expected to be available to students." Our broader dataset revealed that the staff administrator seems to spend the entire work week in the writing center, dealing with the everyday business of running the center. This administrator may spend much of his or her time

Table 3.3. Hours worked per week

Hours Per Week	*Staff n = 42*	*Non-TT Faculty n = 25*	*TT Faculty n = 49*
11 to 20	7.3%	4.2%	0.0%
21 to 30	2.4%	0.0%	2.1%
31 to 40	46.3%	25.0%	14.6%
40 plus	43.9%	70.8%	83.3%

Table 3.4. Location of work

Hours in the Center	*Staff n = 42*	*Non-TT Faculty n = 25*	*TT Faculty n = 49*
All time	45.0%	16.7%	2.1%
2/3 time	20.0%	16.7%	20.8%
1/2 time	5.0%	16.7%	18.8%
1/3 time	12.5%	37.5%	18.8%
Most outside	17.5%	12.5%	39.6%

engaged in the daily operations of the center, including completing and filing paperwork, interacting with tutors and students, conducting trainings and observations, and assessing the effectiveness of the center's services. These administrators may engage in research activity and travel to conferences, but this is not a central expectation of their ongoing work.

The work life of a faculty administrator, however, seems to take that individual outside the writing center on a frequent basis. According to the majority of faculty respondents, off-campus time is often one way they manage the full range and expectations of their activities. Faculty workdays are also filled with work that is vital to the writing center, but this work is defined differently by respondents, who describe more time involved in teaching, leaving the center to attend meetings with campus administrators and other faculty, engagement in cross-curricular initiatives, attending events that allow for relationship building with others on campus, and pursuing a recognizable research agenda. Working at home during evenings and weekends seems to be one way faculty administrators manage workflow, handle deadlines, and keep up with the multiple requirements of their positions.

Thinking strategically about how HR designations organize the work of writing center professionals, we asked both faculty and staff to tell us the most common misconceptions others had about their positions. Respondents in both groups were fairly candid in their responses, noting—unsurprisingly for those familiar with writing center research—that perceptions of them and their work (despite institutional rank) were products of the ever-prevailing notion that writing centers are "fix-it shops" or sites of remediation. Here is where standpoint can help us hone in on how this misrecognition plays out differently in the daily lives of staff and faculty. Respondents who held staff positions noted that they were not recognized as educators by others in their institutions. Examples of staff responses follow.

> I suspect that many administrators and non-English faculty believe that I am an administrator rather than part-administrator, part-teacher. I have as much or more student contact as any instructor, but my title is "supervisor" and I have "staff" status.
>
> * * *
>
> Because I am half-time staff, I do not believe they consider me a professional.
>
> * * *
>
> Administrators don't realize how much teaching and student interaction I have on a daily basis.

Faculty respondents, however, noted more misrecognition of their professional identities among colleagues. Examples of faculty responses follow.

> Some don't realize that I am a tenured professor; some don't realize I work many hours at home.
>
> * * *
>
> [They consider it] "luxurious" release time; [little] awareness of workload and heavy clerical/administrative commitment of [the] center . . . much more than a 0.25 addition to my job/workload.
>
> * * *
>
> Little understanding of what is involved in managing a tutoring program (particularly HR-related tasks and procedures) and the amount of time it takes to adequately develop, implement, and assess the program (including in relation to the institutional Strategic Plan).

This initial foray into understanding the differences staff and faculty HR designations may make in the everyday lives of writing center professionals helped us understand the sorts of questions I might ask when I began to interview and observe the work of writing center administrators and to observe how this work coordinated with the annual review process. Discussions in the field drawing in anecdotal evidence and shared experience have explored at length the differences of rank and prestige writing center professionals experience based on HR designation. Initial survey results bear out the nature of the conversations, confirming that writing center professionals must negotiate their positions in light of the ways their HR designation institutionally positions them.

These survey data established a baseline for a more focused effort to understand how HR designations were playing out in local settings for writing center professionals. Survey responses revealed broad differences in gender, local recognitions, misrecognitions, and locations of work. These responses reveal that faculty and staff professionals expressed comparable concerns over workload expectations and the visibility of the work they carry out. They were very similarly concerned that those they work with might not recognize them as equals, as educators, and as people who engage in work of an intellectual nature. But these survey data also began to uncover the reality that workload expectations and recognitions play out quite differently for staff than they do for faculty. Already, we were uncovering how the HR designations we asked about in the survey coordinated the everyday work of our respondents within their local settings. As I dug more deeply into the annual review process, I continued to see divergent experiences in the coordination of everyday work for staff and faculty writing center administrators.

QUITE DIFFERENT REVIEW PROCESSES FOR STAFF AND FACULTY

> *Texts such as medical charts, enrollment reports, strategic plans, and so on are mechanisms for coordinating activity across many different sites . . . Institutional ethnographies are designed to reveal the organizing power of texts, making visible just how activities in local settings are coordinated and managed extralocally.*
>
> —Marjorie DeVault, "Introduction," *People at Work*

In stage two of this project, I conducted interviews with and collected annual review documentation from writing center professionals in staff and faculty positions at a variety of different-sized and Carnegie-classified institutions. Of these participants, three self-identified as "staff" and three self-identified as "faculty" (tenure track or tenured). My questions during these interviews focused on the administrators' experiences in their positions; how they negotiated the logistics of their positions; how they saw their work in the center reflect institutional histories, missions, and identities; and how they experienced the everyday hierarchies they encountered. Following their interviews, both staff and faculty participants shared copies of their annual performance review forms and described the basic processes with me. The three writing center professionals who were staff shared their private performance review forms and processes. The three faculty participants shared their annual *and* third-year review processes and narratives, noting that that these processes were integral to the possibility of performance increases and their tenure bids.

The contrast between staff and faculty reviews is a fairly revealing entrance point for a conversation about how texts coordinate writing center work. I note the immediate difficulties that come with comparing the annual review process for staff to the third-year review process for faculty—the time frame for and stakes attached to each review process obviously diverge. But ultimately, as the end result of these processes is the renewal of the terms of employment for the individual who holds a contract, the differences between these formal processes offer a telling snapshot of institutional procedures and are suggestive of the ways HR distinction maps to differing institutional values. On the surface, the length of time associated with employment contracts can suggest a different degree of institutional investment in the positions and the work carried out by those who hold those positions. (As one of my faculty respondents shared about a colleague who holds a one-year contract that is renewed annually in the spring, "He can do no longitudinal planning, really, because he's one year to one year. And this goes beyond writing. Sustainability is a huge thing. And we try to do all this stuff with sustainability on our campus, a lot of great projects. His job? One year to one year.")

A few other basic differences and similarities are important. All three of the staff respondents were asked to fill out standard annual review forms that applied to all employees holding positions in similar categories of employment at their institutions. Two of these forms were generic and offered little opportunity for revision of the language and criteria to be used to evaluate the work of the writing center administrators. The forms offered no space to include specific job tasks or professional responsibilities that would be evaluated. Further, because these forms were templates intended for use across a diverse array of positions, they tended to offer fairly generalized language about work activities.

Some interesting commonalities also existed across the two generic forms for staff administrators. One form focused the review on broadly applicable criteria such as "Quality of Work" and a number of specific descriptives, such as "Accuracy (of Work)," "Timeliness," "Dependability," "Technical Competence," and "Attention to Detail." These categories could have been applied to many staff positions on the campus but seemed especially rooted in notions of accountability to a 9-to-5 conception of work and ideals of customer service, opening and closing an office, record keeping, relations with co-workers and clients, and the skills necessary to manage rote work processes. The evaluative focus of these categories included brief descriptions, such as:

- Quality of work: Completing work thoroughly, accurately, neatly, and according to specifications; producing output with minimal errors.
- Quantity of work: Consistently producing a high volume of acceptable work; producing services or output quickly and efficiently.
- Timeliness: Completing tasks and assignments in scheduled time; allocating time to various tasks and assignments in accordance with priorities; informing supervisor when schedule problems occur.
- Use of resources: Making good use of resources, not wasting time or material; looking for ways to reduce costs; staying within budgets allocated.
- Attendance and punctuality: Coming to work regularly without excessive absences; maintaining assigned work schedules.

This language suggests that the staff writing center professional was responsible for following a set of organizational processes and procedures determined by others. Interestingly, despite this prescription of power and work, the form also evaluated the employee's "Initiative: Anticipating problems and voluntarily taking appropriate actions; assuming responsibility for work without being told; seeking out or willingly accepting tough assignments."

Similarly, the generic rubric used to evaluate the other staff writing center professional included these criteria:

- Quality of work: Completes the appropriate amount of work expected.
- Organizational skills: Effectively establishes priorities and schedules, structures tasks, and organizes projects/workflow to achieve maximum efficiencies on schedule. Plans in advance.
- Working relationships with others: Relates effectively and in a welcoming manner with students, parents, colleagues, and/or other visitors to the university. Treats others fairly and respectfully. Consistently seeks win-win solutions. Demonstrates tact and cooperation. Communicates in appropriate manner.
- Problem analysis and problem solving: Ability to evaluate tasks and problems and implement appropriate courses of action. Devises creative, thoughtful, workable, and sound solutions to problems even in time-sensitive or pressured situations. Demonstrates initiative in identifying problems and solutions. Note: Problems can be routine or complex.
- Coaching/development of staff (to be completed by managers for staff in supervisory positions only): Devotes time and effort to coaching staff; provides staff with appropriate feedback, development, or learning opportunities; meets regularly with staff; ensures staff are

informed about university and department goals, initiatives, and policies; encourages an environment that supports staff achievement.

- Leadership (to be completed by managers for staff in supervisory positions only): Demonstrates strategic vision and planning for area of responsibility. Coordinates work and workflow for area to achieve university and department goals. Maintains a positive attitude about administrative decisions. Expresses concerns in an appropriate manner and forum. Motivates and encourages team work within the department and externally.

For this staff writing center administrator, too, the generic form forecloses the development of descriptions for work tasks and expectations. The last two criteria on the form, for instance, clearly ascribe the authority for their completion solely to the "supervisor."

All three forms for all three staff administrators tended to use a numerical scale or a check box system to indicate the supervisor's sense of the employee's quality of work. One review form, for instance, included these three options: "Exceeds Expectations," "Meets Standards," "Does Not Meet Standards." Another staff writing center professional's review looked much like a report card (see figure 3.1), with five categories in the top line of a check box system and a series of weights for the criteria. (The employee did not know what the acronym PMP in the upper left-hand corner stood for.) At the end of the form, these scores were compiled and totaled. This metric was then used to determine "whether [the employee] was eligible to receive any raise that had been declared by the state and university." The employee's work would be rated as "Outstanding," "Above Standards," "Meets Standards," "Below Standards," or "Unsatisfactory." To receive a raise, he needed to "meet standards" in all categories.

Only one of the staff respondents had the option of filling out a form that could be particularized to her position. The form for this staff writing center administrator offered a series of spaces under the broader heading of "Day-to-Day Duties and Responsibilities: How well were these performed." A series of blank fields below this heading on the form allowed the administrator to enter and describe not only her specific activities or goals but also the terms by which her performance might be evaluated. She was then able to describe and focus the process of evaluation on the projects, workflows, and relationships she had developed during the year. Her work was then evaluated using a four-point scale: "Exceeds Expectations," "Meets Expectations," "Needs Improvement," or "Unsatisfactory."

This staff writing center administrator was able to describe in clear and directive terms the scope and purpose of her professional responsibilities

PMP RATINGS WORKSHEET

Employee

Individual Performance Factors			
Factor	**Wgt**	**Rating**	**Wgt x Rating**
Quality of work	2	3	6
Quantity of work	2	4	8
Timeliness	2	4	8
Use of resources	2	4	8
Attend. & punct.	2	3	6
Oral comm..	3	5	15
Written comm.	3	5	15
Coop. & teamwk.	2	4	8
Inter. relat.	2	4	8
Customer service	2	4	8
Public relations	2	3	6
Planning	3	4	12
Problem solving	3	4	12
Creativity	2	3	6
Job knowledge	2	4	8
Handling challenges	2	3	6
Initiative	2	4	8
Administration	2	3	6
Other		0	0
Other		0	0
Sub-Total	40		154

Mgr./Sup. Performance Factors			
Factor	**Wgt**	**Rating**	**Wgt x Rating**
Setting objectives	3	3	9
Budgeting	2	3	6
Org. & wk. allocation	2	3	6
Coordi./Integ.	3	4	12
Monitor. grp. results	3	3	9
Staffing	2	3	6
Def. expectations	2	3	6
Feedbk. & coach.	2	3	6
Perf. reviews	2	3	6
Hum. res. devel.	2	4	8
Leader. & motiva.	3	3	9
Comm. link	3	4	12
Other		0	0
Other		0	0
Sub-Total	29		95

Overall "Score"			
	Wgt		**Wgt x Rating**
Ind. Perf. Fact.	40		154
Mgr./Sup. Perf. Fact.	29		95
Op. Objectives	0		0
Total **(A)**	69	**(B)**	249
CLICK HERE FOR FINAL CALCULATION			
Overall "score" = (B) / (A) =			3.61

Operational Objectives			
Objective	**Wgt**	**Rating**	**Wgt x Rating**
I		0	0
II		0	0
III		0	0
IV		0	0
V		0	0
VI		0	0
Sub-Total	0		0

Overall Performance Rating				
Outstanding	Above Standards	Meets Standards	Below Standards	Unsatisfactory
☐	☑	☐	☐	☐
4.5	3.5	2.5	1.5	

Figure 3.1. Numerical Scorecard

as the "director of peer consultation," breaking tasks into nine discrete and specifically described sub-categories. Examples of the language detailed for evaluation, then, included:

- Design, implement, and facilitate student consultant training for twenty-six students and twenty additional TAs (e.g., produce and maintain training manual in line with national norms; provide oversight of consultant training; organize and lead regular labor meetings that pertain to consultant certification); serve as primary labor supervisor and program administrator.
- Serve as campus consultant on issues pertaining to effective communication and student academic success (e.g., work with the General Education Program's writing courses and teach two writing courses

> per year); consult with faculty on coursework and professional writing; provide annual workshops for creative writing courses; work with the Office of Academic Services and the Special Needs Coordinator to identify students in need of attention by those offices; support faculty in conflict mediation with students; as appropriate, serve on college committees that pertain to student academic success.

The other two staff respondents were not able to change the language of the categories that described their work and had far more restricted opportunities to describe the scope of their daily activities, although the option to place an "N/A" in particular categories was offered to one of the two respondents with less flexible forms.

Even noting the flexibility of one of these three forms, in all cases the forms that evaluated the work of staff writing center administrators tended to reify a process that positioned the supervisor as the evaluative authority over the employee's work. At times, the relationship between the staff writing center administrator and his or her supervisor was constructed by the prescriptive language of the form itself; at others, this relationship was constructed by the design location of the supervisor's comments and the employee's comments or by the omission of language and space on the form to open, engage, or enact a different process or criteria. Two of the evaluation forms offered the supervisor more space to comment on the employee's performance (for instance, a place for the supervisor to comment after every descriptive category and ranking) than for the employee him- or herself to describe or comment on his or her own work. These forms offered little to no opportunity for the supervisor or the employee to revise the tasks and responsibilities that would then be evaluated. One of the staff writing center administrators overcame these difficulties by writing in extensive descriptions and rationales to work against the grain of the original language of the form. But as this professional reported in her interview about her review process experiences, *her supervisor did not respond positively to this tactic.* The other staff writing center administrator with a prescriptive generic form reflected cynically, "I may as well have been a janitor or a groundskeeper."

None of the forms for staff writing center professionals sought information on activities that are often more closely related to conceptions of faculty work, which many writing center administrators who hold staff positions might wish to and often do take up. As a matter of course, these forms did not ask about teaching, honors/awards, scholarly contributions (such as publications), attendance at national or regional conferences, or engagement with a national field. One of the three staff respondents could write this information in and have it included in an area of the form that designated "Other Activities." But for the other two writing center administrators, the most likely area to have this type of information included was "Staff Accomplishments"—which on one form was "To be completed by Supervisor."

In contrast to the generic form all three staff were asked to fill out, only one faculty participant noted having an institutionally generated generic form ("a database," in her language). The other two faculty authored and submitted a flexible but template-driven "annual report" that focused on the three general categories of faculty labor: research, teaching, and service. None of these processes entailed using evaluative language or the proscriptive application of criteria to the work of writing center administrators, as did the forms for staff. Instead, these forms tended toward the simple "reporting" of activities in each category. One interesting difference in the "reporting" of these faculty involved the placement of "teaching" in the organization of the reports; smaller "teaching" institutions (a small branch campus and a small liberal arts college) asked about teaching before asking about other annual activities. Teaching at the two smaller institutions also included advising activities. Reporting for each category necessitated listing the number of publications and projects (including "external grants or other awards," "participation in professional meetings/conferences," and "faculty development") the faculty member had in process or had completed that academic year, the number of courses taught and students advised, "service contributions," and "honors, awards for teaching, advising, scholarly and creative work or service." One participant added a line on his form about "consulting," which included descriptions of outside review work he had participated in.

The most prescriptive review process for faculty was described by a respondent who noted that she "loads" information about her research, teaching, and service into an "Activity Insight Database," which she described as "a system required by the university." The database generates a report that is printed out (and, she mused, is perhaps "counted" by upper administration) before it is sent to the Annual Review Committee, which is made up of senior tenured faculty in the department and the department chair. The committee then generates a "report card," which evaluates the faculty employee's research productivity and engagement in teaching and service on a five-point scale using this terminology: "Extraordinary Performance," "Exceeded Performance Expectations," "Met Performance Expectations," "Below Performance Expectations," and "Unacceptable Performance." The other two faculty administrators noted that they are similarly evaluated but that their universities and departments provide directions for producing a report that follows somewhat standardized conventions. One participant noted that faculty in their department are encouraged to ask peers for examples of their reports to use as models.

Here, we begin to bump against additional issues in the generalized approaches of the annual review processes for writing center administrators who hold faculty appointments. All three tenure-line respondents confided the difficulties of fitting their work into the three typical categories of faculty work: research, teaching, and service. One faculty member noted, for instance, that because 50 percent of her time is reassigned to administrative work that does not fit into the general categories of teaching, scholarship, and administration, her scholarly and teaching output was mistakenly evaluated at the level of "Met Performance Expectations" instead of "Exceeds Performance Expectations." If evaluated by the metrics of her contract (20% teaching, 20% research, 10% service, and 50% administration of the center), she would have been evaluated at the level of "Exceeds Expectations." The system that coordinated this writing center administrator's review process could not account for the differences of her workload set by her contract. So even as her contract stipulated a different distribution, the standard processes for annually evaluating her work were not prepared to take the differences in her work distribution into account.

The other two faculty writing center administrators noted that even without a predetermined "database" to organize their annual review information, the categories the institution offers for evaluation do not always encompass "administrative" activities or aspects of program leadership. The difficulty here, as one respondent noted, is in determining how work as a writing center administrator fits into the institution's understandings of the traditional categories of faculty work. "So, for example," one notes, "the faculty workshop I co-led this summer for science writers. Is that service? Teaching? I try to get as much into teaching as possible because service counts for naught." In a follow-up email, another wrote, "So much of what we do encompasses all of these areas at once. It's difficult to divide them. At my institution, this is understood and I feel that things I did as writing center administrator that were 'all of the above' were valued. An example might be doing collaborative research projects as professional development/training for tutors, research for myself, and also as a way to improve the writing center. But how do I put that on my form? It's a question every time."

These concerns parallel the concerns for recognition, status, and institutional visibility that are active in the field and foregrounded in the responses of survey participants collected in the pilot stages of this project. It seems a telling distinction that the reviews for staff place enormous evaluative power in the hands of a single supervisor, whereas faculty who carry out writing center work are evaluated by a committee of peers. Likewise, it is not easy to dismiss that staff tend to be evaluated for the quality of what they do and faculty tend to be evaluated for the amount they produce. (Of course, faculty evaluations also tend to include student evaluations of the teaching, but even these "evaluative" elements of the review process are mitigated by statements, such as this one that appears on the directions given to the faculty participant from a small branch campus: "Although student evaluations by themselves do not provide sufficient information to validly judge a faculty member's performance as a teacher, they do contribute to the overall faculty evaluation process.")

In looking at these annual review forms, it is no wonder that some have come to the conclusion that staff and faculty carry out their work in entirely different worlds. I talked with each participant to begin to flesh out how they lived these differences.

STAFF AND FACULTY EXPERIENCE THE REVIEW PROCESS

> *Some of my labor is visible to students and some of it is visible to faculty and some of it is visible to deans. But some of it is invisible to students and invisible to faculty. I'm trying to make it more visible to our brand-new dean. A lot of my work is invisible.*
>
> —Staff and Faculty Standpoints Project Participant 2 (interview)

When we listen to staff and faculty writing center administrators discuss the performance review processes for their positions, we begin to see how entrenched processes coordinate the work of these professionals within local hierarchies and institutional value systems. Consider these two examples of the experience of the annual review process:

> **Staff administrator:** So, pretty much, I would just be called into my department chair's office. The review form was already completed, and I might get maybe up to a day to look through it and sign it, essentially. You know, I could go and talk with that person for a little bit about it. But there wasn't much of a process.
>
> **Interviewer:** Was there any opportunity for self-evaluation or to contribute to the conversation about how your work was reviewed or what would be reviewed?
>
> **Staff administrator:** No.

* * *

> **Faculty administrator:** The review process has been interesting. The first year I thought: I have to do this faculty review, and then I have to do this administrative review, so what goes here versus what goes there? And then by the second year I was like: that's not who I am. So one of the things you see in my third-year review is an attempt to resist separating these identities out—my administration and my research go together. I theorize my administration. So that third-year review document is an attempt to change the narrative of the university . . . Because I have that third-year review that is attached to the tenure process, I'm able to push on those institutional narratives.

The staff administrator above described a restricted review process that did not seek much involvement from him or a process that would align the review with the values of the work of a writing center administrator as it has been defined by writing center studies in recent decades. In contrast, the faculty member described a creative and intellectual process that, as she noted, allows her quite a bit of latitude to post and categorize the work that will be evaluated and to push gently against descriptions and processes that may not fit her day-to-day focus. These divergent examples were indicative of how the two groups, staff and faculty, discussed the evaluation process. Faculty respondents noted that their review processes encourage them to think expansively about how their work contributes to local *and national* academic communities, while staff respondents recounted that their reviews were typically about how their supervisors interpreted the quality of their work within almost entirely local contexts. Two of the staff writing center administrators cited above described feeling that the review process did not reflect the "professional" nature of their work or the expertise they brought to their centers from their graduate studies of writing center professional practice and discourse.

Faculty administrators, however, described a more flexible process driven by their own understandings of their work and recognition of professional expertise. They also noted the ways the annual review relates to the third-year review—the annual review tending toward a pro forma process that may or may not connect to yearly merit pay increases and the third-year review closely related to contract renewal. The exegesis of the third-year review document was even looser than that of the annual review. The third-year review tended to offer a snapshot of productivity, but faculty writing center administrators also approached the third-year review as a process that functionally enabled them to explain the nature and value of their everyday work to their faculty peers and supervising administrators. The narratives of these texts tended to assert the faculty writing center administrator's unique professional identity—an identity that aligned with and forwarded the educational and scholarly values of the institution. These review narratives, then, offered faculty writing center professionals the opportunity to demonstrate how their most valued practices aligned their daily work with institutional values.

The creative nature of the process of third-year review is worth noting. None of the faculty interviewed received explicit directions for completing or processing the form. Instead, they tended to receive models of reviews written by peers who had successfully achieved tenure. One faculty administrator explained, for instance, that she faced no length restrictions or further directions around the sort of narrative she was required to compose, beyond the lengths and conventions suggested by the models she was given. This process allowed her to strategically frame the portions of her job that may be less understood or unfamiliar to people outside writing center communities in terms they would understand and perhaps appreciate. She described this as a negotiation that allowed her to showcase exactly how she established expectations for herself and then met those expectations for her work. In later sections of her interview, she also recounted that colleagues in her department reviewed her narrative and offered formative feedback before submission. Colleagues offered her advice on reframing and revising as necessary, offering her the benefit of the institutional knowledge they had gained through the processes of their own reviews and work mentoring other new scholars in the department. As they supported the vision of work the faculty writing center administrator had devised, they supported and encouraged the image she had carefully crafted. The creativity and rhetorical nature of the annual and then third-year review narrative allowed her to persuasively reveal to others how she had taken up the priorities and values of the institution through her everyday work.

Admittedly, the stories recounted by the two individuals who began this section were the most divergent of those in my small sample. Yet other, similar divergences across the responses of study participants are worth noting. Overall, staff writing center administrators discussed the process of the reviews as prescriptive, formulaic, and template-driven (focused on completing the form), with the supervisor setting the tone and metrics at the center of the process. Any changes to these prescriptive processes needed to be negotiated and approved in advance by supervisors and were coordinated by the architectural structures of the boss text—the form itself. For staff, the evaluation forms and processes clearly prescribed a role in an employment hierarchy and dissuaded or limited interactions that did not fit into those restrictions. This process, then, often further reflected on the value of that employee's work within the larger institutional culture. Further, all three staff participants noted that some of the criteria applied to their performance did not seem relevant for the type of work that was a part of their everyday situation; however, these criteria could not be removed from the forms. And none of the forms for staff participants offered attention to teaching (even if the staff writing center professional was teaching classes), encouraged engagement with ideals in the field of writing center studies, or inquired about ongoing scholarly or creative activities. As such, staff forms tended to erase the educational aspects and creative pedagogical grounding that have long been held central to the identity of writing center work and leadership on a national level.

What does it suggest about institutional values when the performance of a writing center administrator is reviewed with the same language that will also be applied to an office clerk, a cashier, a groundskeeper, or a cafeteria worker? By no means do I suggest that staff writing center administrators (or faculty administrators) are in any way superior to these other laborers; my point is simply that generic HR forms elide the sorts of hybrid identities and particularities that have been central to the professionalization of writing center labor in the last few decades. In particular, these forms erase the creative, intellectual, and educational mission at the heart of writing center work regardless of HR designation.

As I note above, the faculty I interviewed recounted creating their annual and third-year narratives in a more freeform manner (typically as a recursive writing process with supportive readership), which allows them to have far more control over what is included in the review process and how their work is rhetorically represented. Most told me, for instance, that they are able to include examples of their published work, annual reports from their centers, student evaluations of the courses they have taught, and other supporting documentation to make a case for their local, regional, and national contributions—an opportunity not typically afforded the staff interviewed. But faculty also recounted that, like the administrator whose interview response begins this section, they often must "push" at received narratives to assert their value to their institutions and colleagues. As one of the faculty participants noted in his interview, "I don't think that deans and other faculty have any understanding about what I do. I understand what they do—I see it. I'd love for them to see some of the magic, the beauty, the creativity, collaboration, and community that happens in this little bitty writing center in the basement."

As such, faculty writing center administrators undergoing annual and third-year reviews face a different set of erasures and coordinating logics. The reviews of these administrators tended to overlook the degree of administrative oversight and program leadership central to their professional work. One faculty writing center professional provided an example of this erasure. In our first meeting, she shared that her position description well matched the ideals that have circulated in the field for a decade, describing each of the categories of her workload (administration, productivity, teaching, and service) as having equal significance. The position had been constructed to recognize the "intellectual nature of [her] work," the writing center administrator told me. But this participant also recounted that when she arrived on campus and began to carry out her work in her first year, it seemed that her senior colleagues and university administrators "[didn't] quite know what to do with [her]" because of the heavy administrative load she carried as the administrator of the growing center. In the first year, her colleagues (some well-established in the field of writing studies and the department) had assured her that they would "go to bat" with the administration when and if necessary to make sure her path to tenure would be secure as she built a vital center on a growing campus.

A month after our final interview, this same participant sent me an unexpected email, writing that she wanted to "update [me] on the conversation with [her chair]" about how to evaluate her administrative work, "which HAS NOT BEEN FORMALLY EVALUATED SINCE I GOT HERE" (*capitals in source text*). She wrote:

> I sort of didn't even realize that 50 percent of my workload was invisible because I was being evaluated under the typical faculty rubric [scholarship, teaching, service]. I just kept trying to weave the narrative of my administrative work into the annual evaluation. HELLO! Shouldn't I have KNOWN better?

You may recognize this individual as the faculty member whose colleagues had evaluated her work at the level of "Meets Expectations" instead of "Exceeds Expectations." In the correspondence that followed, this professional assured me that her chair was "on it," making sure her work was evaluated fairly and in its entirety from that point forward. Yet as I note in the description above, it was not a matter of her colleagues simply adding to the mix the missing administrative work as they reviewed her annual efforts and output; the electronic system her colleagues were required to use had imposed an inflexible set of metrics to her narratives that recognized only the traditional categories of scholarship, teaching, and service. This professional's department chair was required to go to upper administration to argue for appropriate recognition of her time and administrative leadership in the writing center. One wonders what this professional would have done without a chair willing to champion her cause.

Another faculty participant revealed a similar set of erasures of his work in the third-year review process. "When I went up for third-year review," he recounted, "no one called me a writing center administrator. I was a rhetorician. And yeah, I do rhetorical theory, but always in a writing center context." He recounted that colleagues had even advised him casually to talk less about writing and the writing center in his meetings and committee work with faculty across the curriculum. In light of these different visibilities and the value of his work, this participant described actively strategizing to "prepare a face to meet the faces that I meet" (a line he borrows from T. S. Elliot); that is, he is circumspect about how and when he presents himself as a writing center administrator versus a faculty member at large. He clearly noted in his annual review that "writing center work involves teaching, scholarship, and service" as a way to foreground the hybrid nature of the work he does and to ascribe its value within the local community. However, he also worked diligently in each area of the annual review to contextualize his teaching, creative activities, committee work, and work in the writing center in relation to norms in the fields of composition and rhetoric and writing center studies, respectively.

These insights into the review process of staff and faculty mirror the challenges revealed in survey data about the everyday work lives of writing center professionals. When comparing the concerns for misrecognition, the shape of the workday, and other aspects of writing center work, professionals who self-identify as faculty noted that their institutions have multiple, sometimes competing, and fairly expansive expectations for their work. Consider the epigraph that began this chapter, in which the faculty participant I am interviewing jokingly suggests that new writing center administrators should keep different types of shoes handy for their different roles on campus—the work of writing center administrators tends to slip between different ways of categorizing it. The expansiveness and mobility described by the faculty administrators mirror the openness and flexibility in the review process. The review process seems to forgive, if not encourage, the dynamic realization of faculty work.

In notable contrast once more, staff narratives of the experience of the review are far more focused on particular and highly scripted relationships. Staff administrators tell a story of more rote day-to-day activities, more time handling the logistics of the center, and less movement from the center itself. The workday that staff participants recount, like survey participants before them, follows a workflow similar to a business office on campus. The work they are asked to carry out is also often typically constrained to the center itself. As one of the staff writing center administrators I interviewed noted, for instance:

> I try to be in the center myself, here as much as I possibly can. I have to be here. I actually have to have hours listed on my website, on my door, when I am going to be here. And I don't want to say it's checked on, but it's pretty much mandatory. Because our students, because of the demographic, there's a lot of need. So being available to them whenever they are needing something is really important for the culture of this school.

This requirement to be present in the center and the related expectations for "Attendance" and "Punctuality" that we see on review forms seem to constitute an important difference between staff and faculty positions. Faculty annual and third-year reviews do not include questions of punctuality, attendance, or work in one's office. Whereas the annual review process for faculty is flexible to some degree, the annual review process for staff feels stiff, constraining, and authoritarian.

When we begin to consider these everyday relations and practices in light of the ways work is constructed around the boss texts of HR designation and annual review, we can see a series of telling hierarchies and systems of value emerge. While inflected by the local character of their campuses and personal relationships, it seems clear that the work lives of staff and faculty are undeniably constructed by these institutional particularities.

CONCLUSION

> *There's a fairly clear demarcation between staff and faculty here. A lot of staff teach as adjuncts, part-time, but it's always in the evening, kind of on their own time. And I don't feel like it's encouraged; I've actually been discouraged from trying to take on teaching responsibilities, other than the one-credit hour position I teach as the writing center director to train the people.*
>
> —Staff and Faculty Standpoints Project Participant 2 (email exchange)

My work on the distinctions rendered by the boss texts of HR designation and the employment review processes reveals how writing center administrators are struggling to make manifest the values of the field of writing center studies in light of competing local institutional discourses, pedagogical cultures, and professional expectations. Even in positions that are ostensibly set up to work from the value systems that are central to the professional conversations in the field of writing center studies, the institutional mechanisms that review the work of administrators often refuse or resist these alignments, catching writing center professionals between the ideals of their work and the local realities of that work. When we consider the ruling relations that order the field of writing studies against the realities ordering the particular local contexts of these administrators, clear disarticulations emerge between the national and local conversations. Discussions about our work, how we name it, and how it is recognized on a campus may well be an entrenched conversation within the disciplinary communities of writing studies. However, these conversations have not made an enormous difference in the ways writing center work is organized within local, institutional contexts, as these findings have shown. Our scholarly discussions in the field might benefit from further attention to these local realities.

The annual review processes I have uncovered echo the anecdotes and prevailing lore that have long circulated in writing center communities about the prestige of writing center work. The positions writing center professionals hold exhibit clear differences along staff and faculty lines: staff administrators face the erasure of their expertise and belonging to a national community of professionals, and faculty face the erasure of their day-to-day responsibilities for paperwork, supervision, training, and professional development activities. The positions these review processes construct require and enable these individuals to respond to institutional value systems in fairly different ways as well. The review forms for staff seem to position them as engaged in forms of "customer service" and "communication" work over other identities more closely aligned with professional standing in a scholarly field.

To some degree, what ends up counting or not counting in employment review processes factors into how the professionals approach their work. Even when participants noted that they do not think about the annual review throughout the year, as one participant confided, participants demonstrated mindful attention to the limits on their time and the values that were ascribed to their activities on their campuses. This was most evident in whether each participant tended to describe day-to-day activities in relation to the field of writing center studies. Two of the faculty I interviewed noted a heightened awareness of how the daily work they carried out would reflect on them *as professionals who were active in their fields* as that work counted toward their bids for review and promotion. On the flip side, two staff indicated lingering feelings of disenfranchisement from the processes and conversations that ascribed value to their daily work as writing center professionals, noting that the review left them feeling as if the institution did not—perhaps could not—recognize the importance of their work to the students and the university community they served.

This study suggests a need for more methodological intervention using tools like IE and its components, as well as extended efforts to explore the actualities of writing center work as it manifests in local contexts. The implications for broader study of writing studies labor are also clear—what might further study uncover about the organization of our work in other sites of writing? How does our labor take shape as our review processes codify or resist the ideals of the field? What additional questions might we ask about the impact of boss texts, such as HR designation and the annual review process, on the everyday activities and coordination of writing center labor? A lengthier and more grounded study may yet reveal additional concerns about the disjunctions between field discourse and the everyday working actualities of writing center professionals. It is my hope that this chapter and this study's results will entice others to join me in the study of how things happen for writing center professionals—continuing to ground this ongoing conversation in the actualities of lived experience for those who hold different types of positions.

4

MAPPING INFORMATION LITERACY IN A FIRST-YEAR WRITING PROGRAM

Social Relations, Material Conditions, and How Things Happen

> *During the fifteen years since the publication of the* Information Literacy Competency Standards for Higher Education, *academic librarians and their partners in higher education associations have developed learning outcomes, tools, and resources that some institutions have deployed to infuse information literacy concepts and skills into their curricula. However, the rapidly changing higher education environment, along with the dynamic and often uncertain information ecosystem in which all of us work and live, require new attention to be focused on foundational ideas about that ecosystem. Students have a greater role and responsibility in creating new knowledge, in understanding the contours and the changing dynamics of the world of information, and in using information, data, and scholarship ethically. Teaching faculty have a greater responsibility in designing curricula and assignments that foster enhanced engagement with the core ideas about information and scholarship within their disciplines. Librarians have a greater responsibility in identifying core ideas within their own knowledge domain that can extend learning for students, in creating a new cohesive curriculum for information literacy, and in collaborating more extensively with faculty.*
>
> —Association of College and Research Libraries, "Framework for Information Literacy"

I begin this chapter by returning to the snippet drawn from a "think-aloud protocol" with a first-year writing instructor in chapter 1. This respondent is describing her "decision points" as she puts together a handout for student writers engaging in research as part of an assignment. The assignment her students are working on asks them to analyze how discourse communities use texts. About twenty minutes into her think-aloud protocol, she begins a seven-minute process of circling among her handout, her assignment, and the library's website, trying to decipher the connections she might pose for her students as they

DOI: 10.7330/9781607328674.c004

develop "research plans." Finally, she stops this cycle; she isn't finding what she would like on the library website, which seems to her to be "only focused on finding sources." The goals she has for her students in this assignment are different:

> What I'm realizing about situated research practices is that . . . [five-second pause . . . and heavy sigh] . . . if I'm researching a community, there may be some things that are valuable on the library website. But a lot of what will be happening in this research process is that my students will be gathering general information about their communities and specific information about one community . . . and that will lead me outside of the typical realm of academic research.
>
> So I guess the question that comes up for me is, what is academic research? What is it not?
>
> I don't want my students to have to be doing the kind of work a graduate student or a person with a doctorate is doing. I don't think they have the resources to, and it will just make them hate life. So I keep coming around back to—how do I make this process manageable for them? And how do I make it accessible for them?

Compare this response to the response of a second participant describing the decision points that arose when she constructed a handout to assist students in learning MLA citation style:

> I want to pose a series of questions that ask them to use their handbook to find the answers. What I'm hoping that they're learning is that there's a system for documentation—there's a way to look up the answers—it's not a memory thing. There are a host of rules and guidelines that exist so that every time they write something and they bring in someone else, they remember that there is this whole system in place.
>
> I will also hand out something I combined from a Purdue handout, which is plagiarism versus paraphrasing. And I say things like: "it needs to be 90 percent of your own language. You can take turns, but there are moves that are essential here to what they are trying to do—to find, to analyze, to synthesize. But your conversation needs to be in your own language."

The two quotations above reveal only two of the fairly different ways the term *information literacy* opens out in the practices of instructors in a writing program. The two quotations also reveal the difficulties these instructors must negotiate as they seek to encourage and support student writers to become effective researchers. Is information literacy about exploring, evaluating, and understanding the value of texts? Is it about using the texts of others in your own writing? Is information literacy about correctness of citation form? Is it about something else entirely? How might different understandings of the term reveal the influence of social relations and material conditions on the shape of our teaching?

As we see in the first quotation, for one instructor the term is about the practical realities of asking students to conduct independent research. And there's this moment in her response—which is the sort of very interesting "tell" an ethnographic researcher is always looking for—in which the instructor demonstrates deep indecision and frustration. She stops mid-sentence. She releases a long sigh. She cannot complete her thought, and she struggles to verbalize a complex and messy hunch. She seems to be feeling out the edges of what she knows about her desires and weighing them against her perceptions of our institutional setting. Trying to put together a handout helpful for her students who are only just learning about college-level research becomes an exercise in frustration; she has visited the library website multiple times, skimmed the resources there, then questioned herself and her motives as an instructor because what she wants her students to learn doesn't seem to match what the library wants students to learn. The first-year writing program outcomes and professional development conversations on campus have asked her to teach her students about the library holdings on campus; her think-aloud protocol exposes her efforts to negotiate this requirement in her own work.

For the second instructor, information literacy instruction tends to entail more concrete practices with citation style(s), source integration, and familiarity with resources available to writers. But here we also see that the second instructor lays down a "rule" that students should be including "90 percent of [their] own language" in any particular paper they write. She suggests that she learned this rule from an online resource that is frequently trusted by writing instructors—the Purdue Owl online writing lab. We see a different process of negotiation in this response, then, as we witness this instructor negotiating her conceptions of effective writing. Part of this process for the second instructor entails adhering to the sort of adage or "rule" that both teachers and students often turn to in writing classes. Note as well that this instructor slips quickly and easily from a conversation about *the documentation of sources*—suggesting that there are rote templates to be followed when citing—to concerns over *source integration.* From there, she slips from the treatment of citation styles into a concern for plagiarism. Clearly, in this instructor's mind, information literacy encompasses a number of larger concerns and approaches to writing instruction, but these topics are all very closely linked to issues of correctness.

These were the sorts of quandaries that arose in my research when I began to ask how the term *information literacy* shaped instructional practices within a first-year writing program at a mid-sized branch campus

(MSBC) in the eastern United States. When beginning this project, my initial questions were very practical and fairly broad—were we collaborating in the most effective ways with the libraries and librarians on our campus? Were efforts to teach research-writing practices in the program effective? Were instructors actually teaching "research" in the ways we were expected to by stakeholders across campus? Responses to these questions began to reveal a far more complex reality, however—a deeper set of disjunctions and conflicts were simmering just below the surface of the program's conversations about research writing and collaborations with the campus library. Many on our campus were concerned with correctness and viewed the first-year writing program as the front line for teaching students about the production of correct research practices and writing habits. A smaller group of individuals viewed work with undergraduates on library research as an opportunity to talk about the social, situated, and rhetorical nature of writing and research in general. These differences of understanding resulted in dramatically different approaches to information literacy in our first-year writing courses.

As I wondered at the array of different assumptions about writing and writers that seemed to percolate through descriptions of instructional practice around *information literacy*, I noted how often instructors' positions seemed to be entangled with the social investments and material conditions of the campus community. In many ways, the term information literacy presented itself as a malleable shape-shifter (or worse, an empty signifier), so broad that it could at once encompass the practical realities of incredibly divergent classroom practices and so vague that it allowed stakeholders on campus (who often held oppositional values) to buy in to the program's work. Tracing the ways the term enabled individuals to negotiate these values through their teaching revealed the sorts of stories research with IE can enable: we can see how key terms, such as information literacy, enable teaching practices to be coordinated in alignment with the social and material actualities of local settings.

These conversations revealed a number of fault lines in our discussions of teaching practice and uncovered many of the intractable and localized, material conditions that have concerned composition scholars on the national level for decades. In fact, my work with IE illuminated that instructors took up the term *information literacy* to manage the social investments and material conditions that shaped their everyday relations with the broader campus community, enacting personal value systems and understandings of the role of first-year writing in the preparation of student writers as researchers. As such, the data gathered through this project demonstrate what we've long suspected and discussed as writing studies researchers: a yawning gap often exists between what actually happens at a site—an institution, a program, a classroom—and the professional statements, disciplinary conversations, or recent research-based understandings of effective teaching practice. In the end, the very personal concerns of our local faculty—a mix of individual and local sensibilities, institutional memory, and personal experiences—drove the use of the term *information literacy* on our campus.

THE "RULING" WORK OF KEY TERMS: ANALYZING TEACHING FOR *INFORMATION LITERACY*

Key terms have an undeniable coordinating force. Raymond Williams (1976) notes that his efforts to define terms such as "culture," "society," and "science" revealed the ideological force of these terms; he argued that these terms often "bind" thought and action to particular interpretations and social investments, organizing what we see and how we see it. Williams's critique of "key words" resonates with Kenneth Burke's (1970, 188) exploration of a "god-term"—a word of powerful rhetorical influence and symbolic logic that allows for the glossing of a variety of particulars under an organizing concept. Williams's and Burke's critiques demonstrate that some words may act as hyper-charged signifiers, revealing "a tangle of relationships" (Burke 1969, 110). The ideological force of these terms, Burke argued, generalizes particularities and shapes motives, limiting and enabling what can and cannot be thought, as the god-terms reinforce the material privileges that accompany a given social structure. In parsing the power of key words, both Williams and Burke demonstrate that specific terms play a significant role in organizing what people do to align with dominant social relations.

IE holds similarly that key terms operate discursively to create a sense of unity and shared practice within institutional sites. Similar to the boss text, key terms can appear in many places at once and often have the support of many stakeholders across a campus community; they may regulate or organize the actions of numerous people over time and space, lending a sense of sameness to what are in fact *quite diverse actions in the name of a shared goal*. As such, key terms are not simply fixed, direct, or neutral indicators of the type of work taking place within a program, and approaching key terms as discrete sets of beliefs or practices offers an incomplete picture of how values, institutional or program culture, labor concerns, and the identities of instructors play a role in the shaping of practice. As we focus on the material actualities of sites of writing, it is important to understand not just which key terms are most active in those sites but how the most common key terms within a program organize what people do and how they do it.

Tracing key terms is one pathway to understanding how the specific faces of an institution are co-created in the space between larger social discourses and individual standpoints. The array of practices we take up in programs speak to who we are, how we identify, and what we value within the hierarchical structures of the workplace we call "a writing program." As such, a "program" or a "campus" for IE is always a site of contestation, disorder, divergence, and disagreement—created in the interactive tensions between what are loosely related sets of individual practices that live below, but always take shape in relation to, official, institutional, and professional discourse. In this study I approached the key term *information literacy* as a dynamic problematic or "situated point[s] of entry" (LaFrance and Nicolas 2012, 151) into the complex processes of decision-making, spheres of influence, and routine that were the writing program in action. To trace deployment of the term, I collected assignments, institutional documents, and survey, interview, and focus group responses. I analyzed how participants discussed information literacy instruction to identify recurring trends and points of identification or resistance. As disjunctions, divergences, and oppositions are always a given according to IE, I particularly sought to understand how different—and sometimes competing—definitions of a term like *information literacy* circulated through the conversations that constituted our program and what those differences signified to the people who held them.

As I note in chapter 1, because IE is concerned with *how things happen*, it allows us to focus on the choices individuals make as they complete daily tasks and negotiate influential value systems in a workplace. Within the IE model, values, resources, and knowledge formations—such as key terms, like *information literacy*—are never accidental; they reveal powerful *ruling relations* at work, discourses that seek to organize the everyday. But in its focus on *standpoint*, IE also foregrounds the individual, noting that "practice" is the result of individuals mindfully participating in the labor hierarchies, value systems, and notions of prestige or purpose that give shape to work within institutional settings. Because the intricate relationships among discourse, material conditions, and what people do are central to this methodology, IE is a methodology ideally suited for coming to understand our institutional complexities.

Data-collection activities for this project spanned three years and included the survey of adjunct instructors in the program (23 of then

28), observations and notes from collaborative work within the program and with the libraries, a review of relevant documents (assignments, handouts, library resources, and readings), and a series of focus groups (4 total groups with 3 to 5 participants in each) and one-on-one interviews (15 total) with first-year writing instructors and faculty in the disciplines. In surveys, interviews, and focus groups, first-year writing instructors were asked to share basic identifying information (including educational background), their definitions of the term, and whether they invited library staff to work with their classes. First-year writing instructors were also asked to describe any instructional concerns, teaching strategies, and challenges faced when teaching *information literacy*–related skills. Subsequent interviews and focus groups asked participants to look over summarized results from survey data and comment on the initial findings, expanding upon their own original answers and the trends represented.

The constraints on this study are important to note: because this project began with a concern for how the term circulated exclusively in the first-year writing program, librarians and a large sample of faculty outside English were not recruited to participate in the survey, interview, or focus groups. Instead, online source-texts produced by library staff and ongoing public discussions about the collaboration between first-year writing and the library provide the primary (textual and observational) data for this study—field-oriented sources of data that have long been valued within the ethnographic tradition.

All responses, observation notes, and textual data were analyzed for emergent patterns (typically, frequency of response), following the grounded theory model (Glaser 1992; Glaser and Strauss 1967; Strauss and Corbin 1997). Two heuristics central to the secondary analysis of data were "ruling relations" and "standpoint" (Smith 2005). Ruling relations are the norms of doing, being, and knowing that we often take for granted, as they coordinate our lived experiences and practices with the experiences and practice of others in different times and spaces. Standpoint theory holds that "knowledge is always socially situated" (Harding 2004, 7). In the juxtaposition of these terms, IE asks researchers to think about how participants co-construct institutional sites through their daily work. Differences of practice and meaning are always a given in the IE framework; as such, I particularly sought to understand how unique definitions of the term circulated through the many ways of doing, knowing, and being that constituted our program. To ensure the reliability of this study, I triangulated the findings across data collected through participant observation, online survey, interview, focus group, and analysis of documents. As categories of response emerged, initial findings were reassessed and redeveloped to attend to the complexities across datasets.

Here is what I found: tracing (or triangulating) the term as it morphed—resisting, aligning with, or overwriting particular resources, individuals, or structures—as it took shape again in sites of instruction and again in hallway and office conversations, not only was revealing of the deeper values and investments in specific practices alive within the program but also demonstrated the deeper difficulties the program faced. In fact, this study revealed that professional discourses—in the form of the "Association of College and Research Libraries (ACRL) Information Literacy Standards" or the "WPA Outcomes Statement"—held little sway over what actually happened in classrooms or (even) library sessions. A number of other highly local, material concerns drove the teaching practices and conversations indexed by the term. Institutional discourses are powerful and coercive, influencing points of identification, sensibility, and action; but so are social relations and material conditions, a series of everyday actualities that order individual lives in ways that are often taken for granted.

RULING RELATIONS: NATIONAL, DISCIPLINARY, AND PROFESSIONAL TENSIONS

For disciplinary professionals such as WPAs, ruling relations are established norms of professional discourse and discussion, organized by the national organizations, statements, standards, noteworthy publications, and subsequent "best practices" central to the work of particular communities or professional fields. The "WPA Outcomes Statement" and the "ACRL Information Literacy Standards," for instance, offer educators a sense of the ideals of practice and other prevailing sensibilities within an active field of disciplinary practice. As these epistemological frameworks idealize aspects of student learning, these statements also endorse particular types of practice and very particular understandings of our work. When our conversations about practice reference these discursive positions, professionals are laying claim to sanctioned forms of identity, belonging, and practice.

In a national sense, the ACRL established the "ruling" definition of information literacy in 1989, when the organization first indexed the term as a "set of abilities" requiring individuals to "recognize when information is needed and [to] have the ability to locate, evaluate, and use effectively the needed information" (Association of College and Research Libraries 2000). As the ACRL has redeveloped the term over time—in 2000, for instance, publishing a lengthy list of competencies and outcomes for information literacy instruction—the organization has tried to account for the changing landscape of education, especially as technological innovations have altered the nature of library services and ideals of "research" practice at large. Thirty years after the ACRL's original definition was released, librarians, libraries, and library journals continue to lead in the circulation, parsing, and application of the term, often inadvertently reinforcing the campus library as the primary cross-curricular hub for research activity on campuses. (Like the "WPA Outcomes Statement," the "*ACRL Information Literacy Standards*" have been revised substantially. The "Framework for Information Literacy" was filed by the ACRL board in February 2015 and formally adopted in 2016 [Association of College and Research Libraries 2016].)

Despite attempts to import the term into pedagogical conversations about writing and the field of composition (see, for instance, D'Angelo and Maid 2005; Brady et al. 2009 as just two examples of this effort), the term often remains on a track distinct from or parallel to conversations about student writing in composition: absent from lead writing studies journals, perhaps embedded within but not overtly recognized by the current "WPA Outcomes Statement," and missing entirely from the majority of textbooks and most frequently used resources for writing classes. A number of sources published in library sciences venues have treated the resulting structural difficulties of such relationships. Barbara J. D'Angelo and Barry M. Maid (2005) note the "frustrations" and "barriers" that complicate collaboration between library staff and faculty—a result of disciplinary or departmental structures whereby faculty in the disciplines oversee curricular developments and librarians are positioned as consultants. These relationships are further complicated by the low prestige granted library staff and faculty. Claire McGuinness (2006) and Laura Saunders (2012) acknowledge that the conversation about information literacy standards taking place in campus libraries has almost entirely excluded input from faculty across the curriculum. And Donna Maziotti and Teresa Grettano (2011) are very clear about the persistence required to find connections between the "Information Literacy Standards" and the "WPA Outcomes Statement."

Conversely, the field of writing studies has had any number of different critical conversations about what "research" is, how it may best be conducted, and what sorts of instruction students as "researchers" need as they socialize into their fields—a series of ruling contests that shape pedagogical approaches in rather different ways. These conversations can be traced to long-held recursive concerns in the field about the "research paper" (such as Ambrose N. Manning's query in 1961 about whether the "research paper" was "here to stay") and subsequent attempts to more explicitly support student understandings of research as a process. Each decade has seen the rise and popularity of different approaches to work with research in writing courses: in the 1980s, Ken Macrorie's (1988) *I-Search* essay pitched "research" as a form of inquiry or exploration; in the 2000s, Joseph Bizup (2008) argued the benefits of teaching research as a "rhetorical practice," while Elizabeth Wardle (2009) critiqued composition's reliance on "mutt genres," including the generic "research paper" born of the inauthentic contexts of the classroom. In the second decade of the new millennium, the Citation Project team opened eyes with findings that revealed how students actually use sources in their writing (see Howard, Serviss, and Rodrigue 2010; Jamieson and Howard 2011). Each of the arguments and understandings of student practice put pressure on the frameworks of previous eras. Indeed, with such little agreement in the field of writing studies about what constitutes "research" or how students best learn its basic conventions, there is little wonder that the term *information literacy* provides a similarly elastic terrain of complexities, contests, and uncertainties.

IE reveals the power of these disjunctions. The separate histories of these professional bodies, their notions of identity, belonging, and purpose, simply induce the practices of these communities to follow different trajectories. When discourses do not easily align, it is not long before practices collide. It is no surprise, then, that campus communities often find themselves experiencing structural difficulties, issues in program alignment, or conflicts of purpose during collaborative interactions that involve information literacy efforts. Key terms and statements are generated by our national organizations to offer a sense of shared values and to guide our work with student writers on fairly different campuses, but, in fact, these pedagogical tools just as easily become the discursive terrain within which variation and conflict proliferate.

STANDPOINT AND THE LOCAL

Whereas ruling relations are about the shared sensibilities that coordinate notions of (best) practice across time and space (Smith), standpoint recognizes the dynamism of individuals as they negotiate the discursive patterns and highly localized realities of writing programs—an awareness particularly important for WPAs, who must rhetorically negotiate these many different investments on a campus. Individuals are always situated within the material, engaging in highly personal association(s) with institutional histories, memories, and patterns that give character to local settings. Participating in forms of social organization naturalizes the multitudes of practice that imbue a site, entrenching certain practices and attendant belief systems. As such, an individual's social alliances, experiences, and sensibilities play an important role in how that individual negotiates everyday institutional settings (such as classrooms, programs, or departments). Our local practices may or may not reflect the ruling realities prescribed by disciplinary or professional discourses.

Recent research in writing studies has shown that local relationships exert enormous force on the pedagogical investments of instructors in first-year writing programs. Heidi Estrem and E. Shelley Reid (2012) have shown, for instance, that the primary pedagogical influences for TAs as new teachers are the local peers/other TAs with whom they work most closely in graduate programs. Teresa Grettano, Rebecca Ingalls, and Tracy Ann Morse (2013) wrote eloquently about the resistance of faculty in a program to the "WPA Outcomes Statement"—entrenched local values were simply at odds with the statement's value systems. Just as tellingly, Tony Scott and Lil Brannon (2013) expose crucial differences exhibited in approaches to writing assessment between tenure-line faculty and instructors in the same program: TT faculty "established their expertise with their peers through staking out different positions in writing education," while non-TT instructors tended to focus on "the teaching they have done for years in this program" and a "co-constructed" (or consensus-based) sense of what mattered most in student writing. Surface concerns ultimately mattered most in non-TT conversations, while TT faculty favored rhetorical moves, questions of style, or notions of audience (Scott and Brannon 2013, 284). These studies demonstrate the importance for ethnographers who work in institutional locations to account for standpoint. As such, a conversation about how a key term circulates on a particular campus must take into account the many local and individual pressures that shape and inform the term's use in teaching and program building.

In this site of study, local factors persistently shaped conversations about the relationship between information literacy and student writing instruction. The campus where this study occurred had struggled with financial goals following a consistent decline in state funding for over a decade. The material conditions of the campus were particularly dire: classrooms and buildings were in disrepair. As enrollment had grown, new classroom spaces had not; it was difficult for writing classes to book into the nearly obsolete computer classrooms (which had persistent issues connecting to online resources, such as the library website). Instructors often negotiated the limitations of classrooms and digital tools in very creative ways—bringing static screen captures of the library's web pages to class in lieu of real-time online access or putting together extensive step-by-step handouts that described research processes. Programs and staff faced budgetary restrictions and severe cuts. Cutbacks to library faculty lines, staffing, and resources had required that all library faculty, including those who had previously only worked with upper-division students, lead "one-shot" sessions for first-year writing on a steady rotation.

Prevailing campus lore had also held that the university and its admission standards had been in dramatic decline. Faculty at all ranks were frequently heard to lament that the university had "become a community college" and to express dismay that first-year students were not prepared for college-level coursework, especially assignments that included writing and research. These conversations often posed instructors affiliated with the first-year writing course, as well as the program itself, as the gatekeepers and interrogators of student work. Conversations about student deficiencies and the desire that writing instruction focus on policing student texts for adherence to standard academic English often dampened initiatives meant to support student writers over time.

In the course of this study, in fact, senior library faculty vocally asserted that it was the first-year writing program's job, first and foremost, to teach students "grammar" and "how to write complete sentences." Senior library faculty actively voiced disapproval of efforts to update the first-year writing curriculum to teach for transfer or to expand the working definitions of research (beyond the search for sources using the library's website) in the first-year writing program. Librarians expressed dissatisfaction with turning instruction away from "correctness" of form and steadfastly asserted that first-year students were prepared only for the most basic search tools available through the library's website. (A first-year writing instructor came to me one day, visibly shaken, to share that a senior library faculty member had openly criticized a research assignment we were developing collaboratively [on discourse communities] during a library session. "I don't know how I would write a paper like this," the senior librarian is reported to have said to the instructor and her students. "Why would you write a paper like this?")

At the same time the library staff leveled these criticisms against the first-year writing program and the program's efforts to update the research assignments we offered, the English liaison also insistently voiced the desire that "one-shot" sessions become a requirement for all first-year writing classes. As the librarian liaison told me in a meeting to discuss our collaborative interactions, "We need to keep students from going to the reference desk." On the surface, it often appeared that the library staff saw their work with the first-year writing program as a crucial means to controlling how students used the library and its overwhelmed services. These social relations and material conditions inevitably shaped the conversations library faculty had with instructors in the first-year writing program, faculty across campus, and administrators like myself as we discussed how to approach *information literacy*–related teaching practices in first-year writing courses. Indeed, library faculty concerns provided an additional, materially grounded context for conversations about curriculum and coursework.

TRACING INFORMATION LITERACY: DISCIPLINARY, PROFESSIONAL, AND PERSONAL RELATIONSHIPS

> *Historically at the center of the university's intellectual process, the [campus] Library is many things to many people. It is the librarian working with a student in the discovery and evaluation of search methods and knowledge resources. It is the physical building with its collections, it is seating for group study and individual contemplation. It is a virtual space with resources that are accessible at anytime from anywhere.*
>
> —MSBC Library "Vision, Values, and Commitment Statement"

The careful unearthing of ruling relations and exploration of standpoints allowed me to map the very complicated interrelationships proliferating through information literacy instruction on our campus. The examples in this section show individuals personally negotiating the different ideals of the term in relation to their own investments, positions, relationships, and pedagogical leanings within the local landscape.

Understandings of the term were especially demonstrative of anxieties around undergraduate use of the library and the growth of unsanctioned search tools, sources, and practices. For instance, the library—often cited by participants across the curriculum as the "source" of the term on campus—deployed discussions about information literacy in ways that endorsed a prescriptive use of the library and its resources, resonating with the library faculty's ongoing assertion that the library was both central to academic work and under-resourced. Instructors' responses were less cohesive, demonstrating some unevenness of understanding of the term, but they were just as concerned with notions of "correctness," especially as instructors consistently focused

What is Information Literacy?

An information literate person has the ability to:

Define an information need and choose appropriate resources

Examples: Turn a general research topic into a research question
Topic: Thin Slicing
Research Question: How effective is thin slicing as a technique employed during an interview?

Resources: Online catalog may have books that talk about interviewing techniques. These would be geared toward managers, so rather than books that talk about how a person should prepare for an interview, they would be about how to manage people. A good database for journal articles would be Academic Onefile.

Search resources effectively

Examples: Keyword searches could include "thin slicing" or "thin-slicing" as well as related terms such as "decision making", "snap judgements", "first impressions", or "rapid cognition."

Evaluate Information

Look at criteria including: How recent is the source, what kind of article or book is it, who is the audience for the source, does it list it sources (bibliography), how much information is there, the information accurate?

Use information

Are you able to insert the information into your paper strategically to strengthen your arguments or provide examples for clarity?

Cite information correctly

Have you used MLA 7th edition format (or the format specified by the instructor) for your Works Cited page?

Figure 4.1. "ENL 101 Lib Guide"

on information literacy instruction as it prepares student writers to conduct research.

The "ENL 101 Lib Guide"

The MSBC library website provides online resources for student researchers. These resources include lists of area-specific search engines, web pages that offer information or explain key resources, tips and research strategies, and resources for navigating the particularities of the library. The "ENL 101 Lib Guide" (see figure 4.1) was developed by the library's English liaison to support the library sessions offered to first-year writing classes. This guide is organized into tabs that offered first-year writing students a general orientation to the library web page, information on finding books, tips for locating journal articles, and support for using citation styles. But interestingly, the guide also, at the time of this study, offered a tab on "Information Literacy." On this tab, a sidebar asked "What is Information Literacy?" and provided a link to an updated definition of the term on the ACRL website. Those familiar with the ACRL's revision of the original definition of information literacy in the late 1990s and early 2000s (see Association of College and Research Libraries 2000, 2012)—one of the national ruling relations identified in this study—may recognize the descriptions of the sub-skills listed on this tab, as the "Lib Guide" lifts the ACRL language directly and without citation.

The "Lib Guide" is organized by headers, with each header referencing one of the major skill sets central to the ACRL's definition of information literacy, which reads "Information Literacy is the set of skills needed to find, retrieve, analyze, and use information." Beneath the headers, a sentence or paragraph is offered to provide further context, define assumptions, or direct students to practice and resources: "An Information Literate person is able to: Recognize and define the need for information . . . Define an information need and choose appropriate resources . . . Search resources effectively and efficiently . . . Evaluate information . . . Use information . . . [and] Cite information correctly." Further, the broad abilities identified by the ACRL are broken into smaller tasks, such as "choosing and narrowing a topic," "identifying search terms," "asking a series of questions about the sources located," and "strategically strengthening your arguments" with the source(s) found. Beneath each of these subheadings, the site then directs students to local practices such as "key word searches" or local resources, such as the "online catalog" or "books and articles," and the site references the "MLA 7th edition format" (a source about correct citation). For instance, the paragraph under "Resources" reads: "Online catalog may have books that talk about how a person should prepare for an interview, they would be about how to manage people [*sic*]. A good database for journal articles would be Academic OneFile." The paragraph about "Examples" reads: "keyword search could include 'thin slicing' or 'thin-slicing,' as well as related terms such as 'decision making,' 'snap judgments,' 'first impressions,' or 'rapid cognition.'" Because the site was designed to be the background for one-shot library sessions, there is little explanation of any of these terms.

Discussion

In the "Lib Guide," the library's use of the term demonstrates the tensions between the ruling definitions of "information literacy" as a key term in a national, disciplinary, or professional sense and how the term circulates through local value systems at MSBC. The "Lib Guide" enacts this tension as it slips neatly back and forth between the broad abilities and awarenesses central to the definition originally posed by the ACRL (now revised) and highly over-determined nods to student practice (and rote skill sets) that prescribe particular step-by-step processes or resources identified for student use. The inclusion of "information literacy" as a term for students to know and understand on the "Lib Guide" itself is a very interesting choice, for students need not know the definition of the term to engage in research activities or to produce many different forms of research-based writing. Further, in referencing the ACRL, the "Lib Guide" draws on the professional organization as a source of legitimation for this approach, a move that centers the campus library as the source for the "information literate individual." This focus also rhetorically situates the library faculty as the stewards of research and reinforces the library itself as the site that sanctions effective research practices. But while the guide does make direct reference to a portion of the first-year writing curriculum ("thin slicing" from *Blink*, the summer reading), it reduces "sources" to "books and articles" and reifies the MLA sourcebook as the primary source for information about citation practice. These moves reflect values supported by the library faculty, who often foregrounded use of particular types of sources over others and privileged resources that reinforced or prescribed correctness, especially of written conventions. In addition, the guide focuses on very broad (professionally and nationally coordinated) elements of information literacy—a move that elides the particularities of first-year writing practice on research as inquiry and writing as a rhetorical process. In accordance with the IE framework, this identification of the disjunctions between discourse and practice clarified that the university librarians often kept the goals of library faculty in mind when we discussed information literacy.

First-Year Writing Instructors' Definitions, Discussions of Practice

In survey responses and interview questions, adjunct instructors persistently referred to the library and library tools when asked to define "information literacy" or describe their teaching practices related to the term. In survey responses particularly, adjunct faculty respondents frequently noted the importance of teaching students *to find academic/scholarly sources* as the center of their classroom practices related to *information literacy*; that is, a simple majority of adjunct faculty (14 of

Table 4.1. Question 1 survey responses

Question 1: "How do you define information literacy?" (n = 18)	
Find, evaluate, and use	7
Find and evaluate	2
Find and use	2
Evaluate and use	2
Find	3
Evaluate	1
Use	1

23) defined the term *information literacy*, self-selecting the term *find* as a central component of this broad set of abilities.

Table 4.1 represents the recurrence of particular types of terms in the definitions of "information literacy" offered by adjunct faculty in survey responses, showing the prevalence of the descriptor "find." A smattering of instructors do focus solely on terms such as *use* (1 of 23) and *evaluate* (1 of 23) of sources in their definitions. The majority of respondents also defined "information literacy" in ways that coincided with the "Lib Guide's" description of "information literacy" as a "process" (described above). In these definitions, references to "finding" sources typically occurred as the first step in this process. Notably, when describing their teaching practices, these instructors revealed a clear preference for sources located through the campus library. For example, when asked how they teach information literacy–related abilities, a number of instructors included work with the library in their responses:

> I instruct them to use appropriate sources, requiring them to "find information."
>
> * * *
>
> Knowing how to use a search engine. And finding information.
>
> * * *
>
> I take time in my course to help students use the library databases effectively.
>
> * * *
>
> Much of my coursework, especially in the computer lab, focuses on guiding students through the various stages of research, from limiting a topic, to asking questions about that topic; then exploring the databases available through the library subscriptions. For students, organizing their ma-

Table 4.2. Question 5 survey responses

Question 5: "How important is each of the following 'competencies' to students' information literacy abilities?" (n = 23)	
Ethical use of sources (18)	78%
Evaluating information critically (18)	78%
Evaluating sources for credibility (18)	78%
Asking research questions (17)	74%
Ability to integrate sources (17)	74%
Familiarity with library search engines (16)	69%
Appropriate documentation of sources (14)	60%

terial is not so much a problem as evaluating the material they collect through their readings.

Overwhelmingly, in interviews and survey responses, instructors shared that "finding" sources was a key aspect of "information literacy" and that they focused the majority of their classroom discussions around research practice and the completing of assignments on this aspect of the term.

When instructors were asked to rank student competencies associated with information literacy, a fuller picture of teaching for correctness and the role of the library emerged. As table 4.2 shows, 18 of 23 respondents indicated that "ethical use of sources," "evaluating information critically," and "evaluating sources for credibility" were equally weighted concerns. A similar grouping, 17 of 23 faculty, also equally weighted "asking research questions" and the "ability to integrate sources" as their next most important concerns. The next highest response rate indicated that 16 of 23 weighted "familiarity with library search engines" as a key student competency. Further, when prompted to suggest other valuable student competencies, one faculty wrote in "understanding what reference librarians have to offer." On the whole, then, faculty in this first-year writing program very strongly aligned their own definitions of "information literacy" with the definitions supplied by librarians and the library's resources.

Yet another set of tensions became clearer as I continued to triangulate the ways instructors described their understandings of information literacy, discussed the role of the library in their teaching, and talked about their work with students. First-year writing instructors who indicated in survey, interview, and focus group responses that they aligned themselves closely with the library, library staff, and library-based research practices also tended to be more preoccupied with notions of "correctness" in student writing. These instructors often discussed information literacy in terms of how their students failed to meet their expectations. For example, an instructor who responded to the question "How would you characterize the library's support services for your work with students around information literacy?" with positive feedback for the library also noted somewhat glibly in response to a later survey question about the challenges of information literacy instruction, "The library is helpful—Wikipedia not so much!"

On the other hand, first-year writing instructors who affiliated or identified with the field of composition, who had recent experiences in graduate school or continuing education practicums, or who tended to gravitate personally to pedagogies of critical literacy tended to discuss information literacy in relation to the opportunities it afforded them as teachers. These instructors discussed the multiple definitions of the term and an array of possible practices—including research methods not associated with the library or its resources: ethnographic observation, cultural critique, strategic reading, and exploration of the strengths and limitations of tools like Google. Their concern was for the effective support of student researchers (as critical thinkers and problem solvers) rather than particular uses of the library and use of preferred tools. The two groups engaged in quite different discussions and classroom sessions around information literacy.

Overall, survey, interview, and focus group findings revealed that the majority of first-year writing instructors conceived of information literacy as *a fixed, a-rhetorical need to find sources* and believed that it was necessary to *privilege library-based research practices, particularly use of the library's search tools to find "scholarly" or peer-reviewed sources for use in student writing.* This tendency to reduce the term to *searching for certain types of preapproved sources* was overwhelmingly true for those individuals who identified that they learned about the term and its definitions from the campus library and that they valued the library as the primary location of student research. We can see an immediate echo between the library's definition above and the following interview response, for instance:

> **First-Year Writing Faculty 6:** Usually, when I break it down for students, I say "it's steps." Being able to understand the directions, what you're being asked to look for. Being able to find the resources you need to find that information. Being able to gather that information. Being able to process that information. So it's a step-by-step process.

Instructors, like the one cited above, who stated that they strongly valued library-based research also specified that they strongly valued collaboration with campus librarians. This indicated to me the degree to which many faculty felt it was important to demonstrate their shared understanding of the term with others on campus—particularly the library faculty who offered one-shot sessions. Embracing the term, in fact, was one of the ways first-year writing faculty were able to both align their teaching with personal belief systems and also signal their acceptance of and responsiveness to what they perceived as the broader values of the campus community—that students use and learn the value of the library as the center of *correct* research practice.

Interestingly, first-year writing instructors who noted close alignment with the library also tended to exhibit the most anxiety around the availability and reliability of general online sources, students' information-seeking behaviors, and the ability of students to evaluate texts for credibility, avoid plagiarism, and adhere to correctness in citation/documentation of sources. Moreover, instructors who aligned themselves with the library noted that they spent a good amount of time teaching citation practices in their classes. One noted, with frustration: "*We go over the styles extensively and yet they are still confused. It is frustrating for me.*" And another described their challenges in teaching information literacy simply as "*citations, citations, citations.*" These instructors tended to voice the most vehement distaste toward perceived student research behaviors, particularly the use of common online research tools. Google and Wikipedia were common targets for casual vehemence, and a number of responses persistently pitted the library against the internet and internet-based resources, noting, for instance:

> I recognize that most students will rely on Google whenever possible . . .
>
> * * *
>
> Information literacy includes the ability to use technology and databases to find and use relevant information of high quality (not Wikipedia, Google, National Enquirer, bozos-r-us.com).

Moreover, the responses of those who identified their understanding of information literacy in line with the library's understanding tended to characterize students as under-prepared, often resistant to learning about the research practices and tools instructors valued, or simply uninterested in more sanctioned forms of research. For example, one instructor responded:

> They just want to Google crap and then comment poach it in and call it good. They are not interested in learning about their topics (even when they choose them). They simply want to get the paper written as fast as possible.

References to student information-seeking behaviors among this group of instructors were almost entirely negative, revealing that many instructors characterize their students as disinterested, even lazy or careless, researchers. As one instructor noted in a survey response: "Students do not critically evaluate the credibility of sources. They often do not ask good research-based questions despite prodding. Usually they are content to 'dump' information at me, not worrying about synthesizing or analyzing it."

Understanding these standpoints then allowed me to also understand that many instructors approached information literacy instruction in ways that echoed more traditional models of research as a library-based practice. Performing allegiances to these ideals through their discussions of the term also allowed these instructors to manage the unwieldy nature of the term's central supporting concepts—reducing the scope and nature of the conversations to more rote forms of correctness and format. Such moves also aligned their classroom practices with the entrenched value for student correctness at work on our campus.

In contrast, instructors who were more likely to push at or challenge a received definition of "information literacy" often worked to expand their knowledge of different sorts of practices available to them. Consider the following, quite expansive range of responses to questions of what they focused on as instructors of information literacy:

> I think many students feel that they are very information literate because they know how to do a Google search. So I think getting them beyond a simple Google search and getting them to see that there are better ways to search for information. And that includes using Google.
>
> * * *
>
> When I hear other people talk about the term, I hear them talking about going to the library and looking things up. It isn't about the process of inquiry. It isn't about the process of evaluating sources—reflecting on why we use sources.
>
> * * *
>
> Restrictions on types of sources students can use in their papers just seem to end up being counterproductive. Some sources are reliable or relevant or strong, but students have found them on their own—they haven't gone through the library's databases.

Discussion

The responses of faculty instructors in the first-year writing program reveal the emerging complexity of our collective teaching practices and the influences that most shaped those choices for faculty in the program—although, despite the disjunctions I point out here, my intent is less to identify "camps" or to indicate an issue with some "bad faculty" and fewer issues with "good faculty" (or librarians) than to reveal how these faculty aligned their teaching practices with active belief systems, attempted to organize their classroom practices in line with broader campus goals and social alliances, and deployed the term *information literacy* to negotiate relationships with others. The divergence of first-year writing faculty feedback is telling in the ways it reveals the concerns and sensibilities of those who were teaching writing at MSBC at the time of this study.

These findings are also highly revealing of the ways the material conditions of a campus may actively shape the character and nature of teaching practice in ways that belie the sensibilities of professionals in other settings, particularly those who would develop standards and statements about best practice in postsecondary classrooms. The influence of internal and external voices—close local relationships and lengthy histories in specific student cultures, differing types of professional preparation, participation in the events (such as conferences) offered by disciplinary organizations, upper-level graduate work, and a number of other personal factors—made a dramatic difference to individual uptake of information literacy as a key term. Personal involvement in discussions off campus, through professional organizations or venues of professionalization (graduate school, teacher certification, extended professional development programs, or professional presentations), tended to bring new ideas to campus, to infuse the teaching of first-year writing classes with more expansive purposes, and to introduce new interpretations of best practices to MSBC classrooms. Research tools like IE offer writing studies professionals a means of uncovering how these differences play out on the ground so that ongoing conversations about our work and our values may be information-driven.

CONCLUSION: A DATA-DRIVEN PICTURE OF LOCAL ACTUALITIES

As I was completing this study, the ACRL was engaged in its own process of revising the information literacy standards that have been the center of collaborative library work on campuses for a number of years into what is now the "Framework for Information Literacy." Colleagues who kept an ear to this conversation described this process to me as undertaking a "paradigm shift," as "the new Framework seeks to address the interconnected nature of the abilities, practices and dispositions of the student, moving away from the hierarchical and formulaic approach of the current standards" (Association of College and Research Libraries 2015, n.p.). This study reveals that efforts to support students as researchers within first-year writing collaborations will require a paradigm shift for many writing instructors, too. I remain struck by the dramatic differences in approach to teaching information literacy and the loyalties and allegiances revealed by my work in the MSBC first-year writing program.

Louise Phelps (1999, 172–73) once noted that writing programs can have a well-articulated central vision but may still be sites of "tensions and oscillations between order and chaos" and demonstrate "huge disparities and variations among [teaching] experiments." For writing studies researchers, many gains come from tracing these local, social, and material contexts, seeking to understand how these contexts may shape the divergent teaching practices of those who carry out their work in writing programs and classrooms. Mapping exercises informed by IE and similar materialist research frames can help writing studies researchers understand the complexities that underwrite, inform, and give shape to the actualities below generalized representations of curricular initiatives.

The findings included here demonstrate the undeniable influence of local conditions to reshape the pedagogies championed by national standards and statements, underscoring that the social relations and material conditions of our programs are themselves the product of historically situated forces and attitudes that actively shape and reshape larger national and disciplinary discourses into unique and highly localized forms. These mapping exercises can also reveal the actual impact of our national efforts to shape teaching conversations and practices. Without continued attention to how the broader field's pedagogical conversations take shape in the situated contexts of our programs, we are always telling only a portion of the story.

For this project, the realization that people took up the teaching of information literacy toward very different ends for very understandable reasons was a generative moment, particularly for ongoing discussions in campus communities about professional development and the qualifications required to teach in the program. The IE framework's focus on ruling relations helped me understand how the term *information literacy* provided a sense of general continuity for the many different individuals who worked within the first-year writing program. Slowly uncovering local actualities helped me see how the material conditions and histories of our site, in tandem with the many rather different standpoints, not only informed the choices people made but also at times demanded or prescribed those choices as a matter of social investments and belonging. In acknowledging these differences and coming to understand the value systems that supported them, I was positioned to think through how the people I worked with most closely were purposefully negotiating pedagogical opportunities in their classrooms.

Work with IE could provide writing studies researchers in other settings with equally useful and data-driven insights into perpetually thorny administrative questions and issues. The deepening reflective spaces this project opened became the productive sites for thinking forward about what we all gained through continued conversation and more reflective collaboration. As we come to understand how practice (in a classroom, program, or site writ large) is a product of the negotiation of local, socially inflected materialities, this type of research might more effectively frame our national and professional conversations, helping us tell new stories that recognize the actualities of our work in sites of writing.

Conclusion

LOOKING UP, STUDYING UP, STANDING UP

Every time a researcher sits down to write, she must invent the university. I borrow this analogy, of course, from David Bartholomae (1986, 4), who argues that student writers must appropriate ("or be appropriated by") highly specialized discourses and unfamiliar audiences to produce successful writing in college contexts. Bartholomae situates his case beside the work of Linda Flower and Patricia Bizzell to argue that the more familiar students become with the expert processes of negotiating with their readers and the more they understand the typical conventions of writing for academic audiences, the more they are able to respond appropriately to the contexts of the "fictional" space of the college writing classroom. Running through Bartholomae's argument is an implicit acknowledgment that the writing classroom is a space co-constituted through this imaginative act. Each player in the story of student writing—the students themselves, teachers of writing, the discourse communities and communities of practice students will enter, the many stakeholders on campus who hold expectations for student writers, and the general public—contributes to these shared spaces in which writing will occur.

I use Bartholomae's argument as a concluding point because—like effective writing—what we call research, in all its many guises, relies on a complex process of expert imaginings. As John Law (2004, 116) writes, our methodologies do not simply "detect . . . reality," they "amplify" it. Our research doesn't just describe social realities, it creates them. Imaginative acts make manifest our values, our ideals, and our understandings of the social. They reflect and recast our experiences and expectations with people, locations, and professional standards. When we imagine our research practices, we are not only generating the assumptions that will enable us to study sites, people, and practices—we are also imagining the audiences who will receive our work and the grounds upon which we will meet that audience. Our work becomes an

DOI: 10.7330/9781607328674.c005

expression of our varied and developing relationships to these readers and stakeholders.

One of the most powerful imaginative moves of IE is its insistence that we are the institution. In Dorothy Smith's imagining, the institution is a dynamic shape-shifter, co-constituted in the moments when people like us—researchers, teachers, administrators, colleagues, students—carry out their everyday work in highly individualized ways. In making this shift, Smith established new grounds upon which the imaginative act of research may unfold, reorienting the ethnographer toward moments of participation, experience, and practice (over an a-critical collection of "bankable guarantees" [Law 2004, 2]). Much of our research on the social, according to Smith, erases outliers, differences, and disjunctions. Focusing on the actualities of the everyday and how these actualities take shape as knowing people negotiate their work is one way of telling stories that are often dismissed, skipped over, or erased. Further, starting a research project with the intent to uncover what may be hidden brings to visibility the contexts that inform writing, writers, and writing instruction. We must "look up from where we are," according to Smith, in order to conduct ethnographic research in a more informed manner.

It is the act of "looking up" (or "studying up" [Nader 1972]) that allows us to re-see the institution and to recognize ourselves as an integral part of the dynamic whole. This reframing allows us to explore key terms with an eye toward praxis. It allows us to imagine new terrains and research practices. It allows us to re-imagine the webs of relationships and values that orient, sustain, and give shape to our questions and modes of analysis. In her similar act of imaginative inversion, Krista Ratcliffe reminds us that these sorts of moves are central to producing scholarship that is ethical and reflective of multiple perspectives and experiences. The act of listening—a central component of all ethnographic practice—defamiliarizes our typical notions of "understanding," positioning the researcher-as-listener in a stance of self-reflexive "standing under" (Ratcliffe 1999, 205). This inversion requires that we become mindful of how discourse positions the researcher and others "while consciously acknowledging all our particular and fluid standpoints" (1999, 205). "Understanding means listening to discourse is not for intent but with intent—with the intent to understand not just the claims but the rhetorical negotiations of understanding as well" (1999, 206). With "standing under" (*qua* "looking up" or "studying up") as a foundational imaginative act, we begin to pay attention to more than simply what is happening, and we key into how what is happening takes shape as a reflection of the social.

But most important, IE also foregrounds that our real work is always relational—always partial, always "understood" through unique standpoints. Inspired by Donna Qualley's reading of a poem about six Indonesian blind men encountering an elephant, which Qualley asserts is "a metaphor for reflexive inquiry," Michelle Miley (2017, 111) argues that the focus IE places on relationality is one of the most powerful gifts of IE. As each man narrates his understanding of an elephant in this poem (one describes the trunk, another the leg, another the tail, and so on), each also insists that his limited experience of the elephant is the right one. Miley (2017, 111) quotes Qualley: "Rarely are we ever positioned to see the elephant in its entirety or complexity during our first isolated encounter with it, but rarely are we taught to acknowledge the limits of initial perspectives." Miley argues that IE's inquiry into the coordination of our work allows us to imagine an institution that is knowable in similar fashion: as we uncover diverse and divergent experiences that are also closely related, if not inter-reliant, we uncover aspects of our interactions—the decisions, alignments, resistances, and moments of practice—that are hidden to the intermittent eye. IE resists the "monologic interpretive scheme[s]" central to the work of much research in writing studies because, Miley (2017, 110) writes, it "embrace[s] the dialogic, the multiple experiences and knowledges that may exist within an organization."

"Ethnography is subversive," Wendy Bishop asserts. Because it requires the ethnographer to imagine a site of study as a field of relational meaning making, ethnography "challenges the dominant positivist view of making knowledge" (Bishop 1992, 152). "It demands attention to human subjectivity and allows for author-saturated reconstructions and examinations of a world; in fact, it is grounded by definition in phenomenological understandings of knowledge and meaning making" (Bishop 1992, 152). IE's recognition of relationality amplifies this call to see our research as an imaginative act that is subversive—an act of rhetorical listening (or "stand[ing] under") with the potential to create a new series of conditions and recognitions. In its assertion that we co-constitute the world in which we live and work and in its re-imagining of the institution as a site that is ready for intervention, IE offers us a crucial reminder of our responsibilities, our power, our ability to resist, and our ability to listen and respect others—even those who are dramatically different from ourselves. It reminds us that solving problems and making change are often a long game, requiring buy-in, relationship building, communication across differences, and mutual respect.

The case studies I have shared here make visible similar materialities of experience and practice that have been missing in the field's conversations about our work. My work with the linked gateway, for instance, revealed that the work processes of the collaborative site (structured as they were by reified forms of labor, questions of disciplinary expertise, and challenging logistics) held enormous influence over the ways writing could be taught, often crowding out established forms of writing instruction or agreed-upon pedagogical centers. The actualities of pedagogical practice, I disclose, while often initially driven by national conversations of best practice and scholarly concern, take actual shape in relation to a number of shifting material conditions and systems of value—a recognition often missing in our field's conversations about effective writing pedagogy. My case study of how HR designations and annual review processes coordinate the work of writing center administrators offers a similar understanding of how local texts generalize (and so erase) the particularities of work for some writing studies professionals. The realizations of this case study extend ongoing conversations in the field about professional status, shedding light on why the field's discourses may not penetrate the local settings of our work as deeply as we might hope. Finally, my work on the key term *information literacy* makes visible the ways a valued term may circulate within campus communities, eliding the many disjunctions of practice that proliferate in classrooms, hallway conversations, and cross-campus collaborations. These findings challenge idealized notions of pedagogy, work, and key terms in our field's discourses. Each of these studies reveals the power of the local, offering writing studies researchers insights into how the field's research might more adequately account for dispersed contexts, divergent experiences, and an inevitable range of practices. When our research reveals more about the material relations we are negotiating locally, we begin to see how our work is co-constituted in actuality. We are able to see where the macro and the micro intersect, coordinating our work across time and space in relation to the work that others do. We are able to seek out the spaces where change may take hold and strategize effectively for the actualities we would like to see.

The many realizations revealed by our work with IE can also be radically reorienting. As we uncover perspectives that diverge from, counter, or resist our own, we are positioned to make more thoughtful decisions as administrative leaders, to identify difficult but important next steps in our curricular and professional agendas, and to more effectively honor those who conceive of our work differently. We are in an era where it seems Pollyannaish to present our work as transformational or subversive. Yet I am moved to acknowledge the simple need for better listening and more understanding within our own institutional communities. I argue in this book that the cultivation of IE for use in writing studies will enable us to deeply explore the material actualities that shape our work. Indeed, IE offers a set of simple tools that are adaptable, scalable, and useful for unpacking local contexts. In the age of austerity, faculty who work closely with writers, writing instruction, and sites of writing need exactly these types of tools and strategies to help us understand the realities of our work and our labor, tools that help us recognize the vital relationships between our field's ideals and what we actually do.

Austerity has been an undeniable and increasing presence for many in the field and in postsecondary education at large, but our means for studying its impacts have also often been limited by our assumptions and investments as researchers. As institutional ethnographers imagine the institution—always in motion, always co-constituted or taking shape *in relation to*—we see ourselves and those we work with as part of a dynamic, interconnected whole. As we continue conversations about how IE may enable us to tell stories differently, to uncover what can only be seen when we "look up," "study up," or "stand under," we are also discussing how it is that our research prepares us *to act* alongside others. We are preparing ourselves to address the challenges and opportunities facing our students, our colleagues, and the sites of writing that are our homes.

We imagine the institution as a locus for possibility and change.

NOTES

INTRODUCTION: TWENTY-FIRST-CENTURY EXIGENCIES

1. For those interested in histories of the use and development of ethnography in writing studies, I recommend Sheridan (2012); Chiseri-Strater (2012); Stinnett (2012). These essays sketch historical developments and critical questions that have dominated the field's discussion around ethnography.
2. Notably, "institution" does not appear in Heilker and Vanderberg's *Keywords in Writing Studies* (2015), released almost two decades after *Keywords in Composition Studies* (1996).
3. Strangely, in "Critical Ethnography, Ethics, and Work: Rearticulating Labor," Bruce Horner (2002, 561) argues that a "cultural materialist perspective on the work of critical ethnography" resituates the work of ethnography "in the material social circumstances" and takes into account the "material consequences for those living at the research 'site.'" An institutional ethnographer would push on Horner's understanding of ethnography and materialist critique, as his work does not attend to the actualities of sites, tending instead to trace broader patterns in the field's discussions and the organization of our disciplinary work.

CHAPTER 1: INSTITUTIONAL ETHNOGRAPHY

1. Smith (2005, 10) herself often problematized her uncritical association with feminist standpoint theory. In fact, Smith eschews the term *feminist* standpoint and instead chooses to use *women's* standpoint because for her, "feminist" standpoint is too restrictive, too essentialized, too loaded with political baggage (a structural sense of gender and class that is itself a problematic). For Smith (2005, 25), "The project of inquiry from women's standpoint begins in the local actualities of people's lives" and is concerned with the "doings of actual people situated in particular sites at particular times."
2. Smith cautions researchers against accepting their initial presumptions of a setting before a study has even begun; our preconceived ideals about organizational standards, forms, and relationships may not bear out in actuality or may perhaps erase important understandings of what is actually happening. She calls these presumptions "blob ontology," a sociological process of assuming that "for every concept out there, there is taken to be something out there that corresponds to it" (Smith 2005, 56). Smith (2005, 163) elaborates, "Social organization is not a concept imposed externally on and used to interpret data; rather, the concept is to explicate what is discovered in the process of assembling work knowledges and finding out how they articulate to and coordinate with one another." The institutional ethnographer must be watchful of going into a research study already armed with concepts or seeking to make the realities they will witness fit preconceived ideals of experience and practice (Smith 2001, 160).

CHAPTER 2: HOW WORK TAKES SHAPE

1. The English department in which this study was conducted is representative of large departments at major state research universities; it offers undergraduate and graduate degrees in literature, writing, theory, and culture. In 2007, the department employed 67 active faculty (6 of these in the composition/rhetoric concentration) and enrolled 669 undergraduate majors and 205 graduate students. Like many large departments of English at R1 universities, the study of literature is central to the identity of the department and the professional practices of most of its faculty. Faculty specializations in the department reflect the broad range of interests in the field at large today ("College of Arts and Sciences Fact Sheet: English," February 2008).
2. A number of scholarly monographs and anthologies have addressed the nature of "incoherence" among sub-fields within English studies: Elbow (1990); Raymond (1996); and, more recently, Downing, Hurlbert, and Mathieu (2002); McComiskey (2006). Many of these texts take up the idea, as Avrom Fleishman (1998, 60) argues, that English departments have been mired in an ongoing search for identity: "An unintended consequence of the pluralist effort to conciliate English's contentiousness is to acknowledge the empty center of the field's sense of itself."

REFERENCES

Adler-Kassner, Linda, and Elizabeth Wardle. 2015. *Naming What We Know: Threshold Concepts of Writing Studies.* Louisville: University Press of Colorado.

Anson, Chris M., and Robert L. Brown Jr. 1999. "Subject to Interpretation: The Role of Research in Writing Programs and Its Relationship to the Politics of Administration in Higher Education." In *The Writing Program Administrator as Researcher: Inquiry in Action and Reflection,* ed. Shirley K. Rose and Irwin Wiser, 141–52. Portsmouth, NH: Boynton.

Apple, Michael W. 2004. *Ideology and Curriculum.* New York: Routledge.

Association of College and Research Libraries. 2000. "Information Literacy Competency Standards for Higher Education." American Library Association. https://alair.ala.org/bitstream/handle/11213/7668/ACRL%20Information%20Literacy%20Competency%20Standards%20for%20Higher%20Education.pdf?sequence=1&isAllowed=y.

Association of College Research Libraries Information Literacy Competency Standards Review Task Force. 2012. "Task Force Recommendations." Association of College Research Libraries. http://www.ala.org/acrl/sites/ala.org.acrl/files/content/standards/ils_recomm.pdf.

Association of College and Research Libraries. 2016. "Framework for Information Literacy." http://www.ala.org/acrl/standards/ilframework.

Bartholomae, David. 1986. "Inventing the University." *Journal of Basic Writing* 5 (1): 4–23.

Bazerman, Charles. 1988. *Shaping Written Knowledge: (Rhetoric of the Human).* Madison: University of Wisconsin Press.

Bazerman, Charles, and Paul Prior. 2003. *What Writing Does and How It Does It: An Introduction to Analyzing Texts and Textual Practices.* London: Routledge.

Bazerman, Charles, and David Russell. 2002. "What Is Not Institutionally Visible Does Not Count." In *Writing Selves/Writing Societies: Research from Activity Perspectives,* ed. Charles Bazerman, and David Russell, 1–6. Fort Collins, CO: WAC Clearinghouse.

Berkenkotter, Carol, and Thomas N. Huckin. 2016. *Genre Knowledge in Disciplinary Communication: Cognition/Culture/Power.* London: Routledge.

Berlin, James A. 1982. "Contemporary Composition: The Major Pedagogical Theories." *College English* 44 (8): 765–77.

Bisaillon, Laura. 2012. "An Analytic Glossary to Social Inquiry Using Institutional and Political Activist Ethnography." *International Journal of Qualitative Methods* 11 (5): 607–27.

Bishop, Wendy. 1992. "I-Witnessing in Composition: Turning Ethnographic Data into Narratives." *Rhetoric Review* 11 (1): 147–58.

Bishop, Wendy. 1999. *Ethnographic Writing Research: Writing It Down, Writing It Up, and Reading It.* Portsmouth, NH: Heinemann.

Bizup, Joseph. 2008. "BEAM: A Rhetorical Vocabulary for Teaching Research-Based Writing." *Rhetoric Review* 27 (1): 72–86.

Bousquet, Marc, Tony Scott, and Leo Parascondola. 2004. *Tenured Bosses and Disposable Teachers: Writing Instruction in the Managed University.* Carbondale: Southern Illinois University Press.

Brady, Laura, Nathalie Singh-Corcoran, Jo Ann Dadisman, and Kelly Diamond. 2009. "A Collaborative Approach to Information Literacy: First-Year Composition, Writing Center, and Library Partnerships at West Virginia University." *Composition Forum* 19: 1–18.

DOI: 10.7330/9781607328674.c006

Brandt, Deborah. 1998. "Sponsors of Literacy." *College Composition and Communication* 49 (2): 165–85.

Brandt, Deborah. 2014. *The Rise of Writing: Redefining Mass Literacy*. Cambridge: Cambridge University Press.

Brodkey, Linda. 1987a. *Academic Writing as Social Practice*. Philadelphia: Temple University Press.

Brodkey, Linda. 1987b. "Writing Ethnographic Narratives." *Written Communication* 4 (1): 25–50.

Brotman, Shari. 2000. "An Institutional Ethnography of Elder Care: Understanding Access from the Standpoint of Ethnic and 'Racial' Minority Women." PhD dissertation, University of Toronto, Canada. http://www.collectionscanada.gc.ca/obj/s4/f2/dsk2/ftp03/NQ50005.pdf.

Brown, Stephen Gilbert, and Sidney I. Dobrin. 2004. *Ethnography Unbound: From Theory Shock to Critical Praxis*. Albany: State University of New York Press.

Burke, Kenneth. 1969. *A Grammar of Motives*. Berkeley: University of California Press.

Burke, Kenneth. 1970. *The Rhetoric of Religion: Studies in Logology*, vol. 188. Berkeley: University of California Press.

Campbell, Elizabeth A. 2011. "Being and Writing with Others: On the Possibilities of an Ethnographic Composition Pedagogy." PhD dissertation, Indiana University of Pennsylvania, Indiana (PA).

Campbell, Marie. 2003. "Dorothy Smith and Knowing the World We Live In." *Journal of Sociology and Social Welfare* 30 (1): 3–22.

Campbell, Marie, and Frances Gregor. 2002. *Mapping Social Relations: A Primer in Doing Institutional Ethnography*. Walnut Creek, CA: Altamira.

Caswell, Nicole, Jackie Grutsch McKinney, and Rebecca Jackson. 2016. *The Working Lives of New Writing Center Directors*. Boulder: University Press of Colorado.

CCCC Executive Committee. 1989. "The Principles for the Postsecondary Teaching of Writing." *College Composition and Communication* 40 (3): 329–36.

Chace, William M. 2009. "The Decline of the English Department: How It Happened and What Could Be Done to Reverse It." *American Scholar*. https://theamericanscholar.org/the-decline-of-the-english-department/#.

Chiseri-Strater, Elizabeth. 2012. "'What Goes on Here?' The Uses of Ethnography in Composition Studies." In *Exploring Composition Studies: Sites, Issues, and Perspectives*, ed. Kelly Ritter and Paul Matsuda, 199–210. Logan: Utah State University Press.

Cintron, Ralph. 2002. "The Timidities of Ethnography: A Response to Bruce Horner." *JAC: Journal of Advanced Composition* 22 (4): 934–43.

Cooper, Marilyn. 1986. "The Ecology of Writing." *College English* 48 (4): 364–75.

Cox, Anicca, Tim Dougherty, Seth Kahn, Michelle LaFrance, and Amy Lynch-Biniek. 2016. "The Indianapolis Resolution: Responding to Twenty-First-Century Exigencies/Political Economies of Composition Labor." *College Composition and Communication* 68 (1): 38–67.

Crowley, Sharon. 1998. *Composition in the University: Historical and Polemical Essays*. Pittsburgh: University of Pittsburgh Press.

Cushman, Ellen. 1999. "Critical Literacy and Institutional Language." *Research in the Teaching of English* 33 (3): 245–74.

D'Angelo, Barbara J., and Barry M. Maid. 2005. "Beyond Instruction: Integrating Library Service in Support of Information Literacy." *Internet Reference Services Quarterly* 9 (1–2): 55–63.

DeVault, Marjorie L. 2008. "Introduction." In *People at Work: Life, Power, and Social Inclusion in the New Economy*, ed. Marjorie L. DeVault, 1–22. New York: New York University Press.

DeVault, Marjorie L. 2013. "Institutional Ethnography." *Contemporary Sociology: A Journal of Reviews* 42 (3): 332–40.

DeVault, Marjorie L., and Glenda Gross. 2012. "Feminist Qualitative Interviewing: Experience, Talk, and Knowledge." In *Handbook of Feminist Research: Theory and Praxis*, ed. Sharlene Nagy Hesse-Biber, 173–97. Thousand Oaks, CA: Sage.

DeVault, Marjorie L., and Liza McCoy. 2006. "Institutional Ethnography: Using Interviews to Investigate Ruling Relations." In *Institutional Ethnography as Practice*, ed. Dorothy E. Smith, 15–43. London: Rowman and Littlefield.

Downing, David B., Claude Mark Hurlbert, and Paula Mathieu. 2002. *Beyond English, Inc.: Curricular Reform in a Global Economy*. Portsmouth, NH: Heinemann.

Elbow, Peter. 1990. *What Is English?* New York: Modern Language Association of America.

Elliott, M. A. 1990. "Writing Center Directors: Why Faculty Status Fits." *Writing Lab Newsletter* 14 (2): 1–4.

Ervin, Elizabeth. 1996. "Institution." In *Keywords in Composition Studies*, ed. Paul Heilker and Peter Vandenberg, 124–27. Portsmouth, NH: Heinemann.

Estrem, Heidi, and E. Shelley Reid. 2012. "What New Writing Teachers Talk about When They Talk about Teaching." *Pedagogy* 12 (3): 449–80.

Fleishman, Avrom. 1998. *The Condition of English: Literary Studies in a Changing Culture*. Walnut Creek, CA: Greenwood Publishing Group.

Gee, James Paul. 1997. "The New Literacy Studies: From 'Socially Situated' to the Work of the Social." Situated Literacies Conference. University of Lancaster. July 8. http://jamespaulgee.com/pdfs/The%20New%20Literacy%20Studies%20and%20the%20Social%20Turn.pdf.

Geertz, Clifford. 1998. "Deep Hanging Out." *New York Review of Books*. October 22. http://www.nybooks.com/articles/1998/10/22/deep-hanging-out/.

Geller, Anne Ellen, and Harry Denny. 2013. "Of Ladybugs, Low Status, and Loving the Job: Writing Center Professionals Navigating Their Careers." *Writing Center Journal* 33, no. 1: 96–129.

Glaser, Barney G. 1992. *Emergence vs. Forcing: Basics of Grounded Theory Analysis*. Mill Valley, CA: Sociology Press.

Glaser, Barney G., and Anselm L. Strauss. 1967. *The Discovery of Grounded Theory: Strategies for Qualitative Research*. Chicago: Aldine.

Graff, Gerald. 2009. "It's Time to End 'Courseocentrism.'" *Inside Higher Ed*. January 13. https://www.insidehighered.com/views/2009/01/13/its-time-end-courseocentrism.

Gramsci, Antonio. 1971. *Selections from the Prison Notebooks*. New York: International Publishers.

Grettano, Teresa, Rebecca Ingalls, and Tracy Ann Morse. 2013. "The Perilous Vision of the Outcomes Statement." In *The WPA Outcomes Statement: A Decade Later*, ed. Nicholas N. Behm, Gregory R. Glau, Deborah H. Holdstein, Duane Roen, and Edward M. White, 45–57. Anderson, SC: Parlor.

Griffith, Alison I., and Dorothy E. Smith. 1987. "Constructing Cultural Knowledge: Mothering as Discourse." *Women and Education: A Canadian Perspective* 3 (1): 87–103.

Griffith, Alison I., and Dorothy E. Smith. 2014. *Under New Public Management: Institutional Ethnographies of Changing Front-Line Work*. Toronto: University of Toronto Press.

Hairston, Maxine. 1985. "Breaking Our Bonds and Reaffirming Our Connections." *College Composition and Communication* 36 (3): 272–82.

Hall, Stuart. 1985. "Signification, Representation, Ideology: Althusser and the Post-Structuralist Debate." *Critical Studies in Mass Communication* 2 (2): 91–114.

Hansen, Kristine. 1995. "Face to Face with Part-Timers: Ethics and the Professionalization of Writing Faculties." In *Resituating Writing: Constructing and Administering Writing Programs*, ed. Joseph Janangelo and Kristine Hansen, 23–45. Portsmouth, NH: Heinemann.

Haraway, Donna. 1988. "Situated Knowledges: The Science Question in Feminism and the Privilege of Partial Perspective." *Feminist Studies* 14 (3): 575–99.

Harding, Sandra. 2004. "Introduction: Standpoint Theory as a Site of Political, Philosophic, and Scientific Debate." In *Feminist Standpoint Theory Reader: Intellectual and Political Controversies*, ed. Sandra Harding, 1–15. New York: Routledge.

Harrington, Susanmarie, Rita Malencyzk, Irv Peckham, Keith Rhodes, and Kathleen Blake Yancey. 2001. "WPA Outcomes Statement for First-Year Composition." *College English* 63 (3): 321–25.

Harris, Joseph. 2000. "Meet the New Boss, Same as the Old Boss: Class Consciousness in Composition." *College Composition and Communication* 52 (1): 43–68.

Harris, Muriel. 1990. "What's Up and What's In: Trends and Traditions in Writing Centers." *Writing Center Journal* 11 (1): 15–25.

Harris, Muriel. 2002. "Writing Center Administration: Making Local, Institutional Knowledge in Our Writing Centers." In *Writing Center Research: Extending the Conversation*, ed. Paula Gillespie, Alice Gillam, Lady Falls Brown, and Byron Stay, 75–89. Mahwah, NJ: Lawrence Erlbaum.

Haswell, Richard H. 2005. "NCTE/CCCC's Recent War on Scholarship." *Written Communication* 22 (2): 198–223.

Healy, Dave. 1995. "Writing Center Directors: An Emerging Portrait of the Profession." *WPA: Writing Program Administration* 18 (3): 26–43.

Heilker, Paul, and Peter Vandenberg. 1996. *Keywords in Composition Studies*. Portsmouth, NH: Boynton/Cook.

Heilker, Paul, and Peter Vandenberg. 2015. *Keywords in Writing Studies*. Boulder: University Press of Colorado.

Herndl, Carl G. 1991. "Writing Ethnography: Representation, Rhetoric, and Institutional Practices." *College English* 53 (3): 320–32.

Horner, Bruce. 2000. *Terms of Work for Composition: A Materialist Critique*. Albany: State University of New York Press.

Horner, Bruce. 2002. "Critical Ethnography, Ethics, and Work: Rearticulating Labor." *JAC: Journal of Advanced Composition* 22 (3): 561–84.

Horner, Bruce. 2016. *Rewriting Composition: Terms of Exchange*. Carbondale: Southern Illinois University Press.

Howard, Rebecca Moore, Tricia Serviss, and Tanya K. Rodrigue. 2010. "Writing from Sources, Writing from Sentences." *Writing and Pedagogy* 2 (2): 177–92.

Ianetta, Melissa, Linda Bergmann, Lauren Fitzgerald, Carol Peterson Haviland, Lisa Lebduska, and Mary Wilsock. 2006. "Polylog: Are Writing Center Directors Writing Program Administrators?" *Composition Studies* 34 (2): 11–42.

Jamieson, Sandra, and Rebecca M. Howard. 2011. "The Citation Project: Preventing Plagiarism, Teaching Writing." http://site.citationproject.net/publications-and-presentations/publications/.

Johanek, Cindy. 2000. *Composing Research: A Contextualist Paradigm for Rhetoric and Composition*. Logan: Utah State University Press.

Kent, Thomas. 1999. *Post-Process Theory: Beyond the Writing-Process Paradigm*. Carbondale: Southern Illinois University Press.

Kirsch, Gesa. 1988. "Writing across the Curriculum: The Program at Third College, University of California, San Diego." *Writing Program Administration* 12: 47–55.

Kirsch, Gesa, and Patricia A. Sullivan. 1992. *Methods and Methodology in Composition Research*. Carbondale: Southern Illinois University Press.

Kleine, Michael. 1990. "Beyond Triangulation: Ethnography, Writing, and Rhetoric." *JAC: Journal of Advanced Composition* 10 (1): 117–25.

Krebs, Paula M. 2003. "The Faculty-Staff Divide." *Chronicle of Higher Education* 50 (12): B5.

LaFrance, Michelle. 2010. "Linked Writing Courses (WPA-CompPile Research Bibliographies, no. 14)." *WPA-CompPile Research Bibliographies*. http://comppile.org/wpa/bibliographies/Bib14/LaFrance.pdf.

LaFrance, Michelle, and Melissa Nicolas. 2012. "Institutional Ethnography as Materialist Framework for Writing Program Research and the Faculty-Staff Work Standpoints Project." *College Composition and Communication* 64 (1): 130–50.

LaFrance, Michelle, and Melissa Nicolas. 2013. "What's Your Frequency? Preliminary Results of a Survey on Faculty and Staff Perspectives on Their Work in Writing Centers." *Writing Lab Newsletter* 37 (5): 10–13.

Lauer, Janice M., and J. William Asher. 1988. *Composition Research: Empirical Designs*. New York: Oxford University Press.

Law, John. 2004. *After Method: Mess in Social Science Research*. New York: Routledge.

Lerner, Neal. 2000. "Confessions of a First-Time Writing Center Director." *Writing Center Journal* 21 (1): 29–48.

Liebson, Rebecca. 2017. "Writing and Rhetoric Professors Face the Realities of Personnel Cuts." *The Statesman*. November 7. http://www.sbstatesman.com/2017/11/07/writing-and-rhetoric-professors-face-the-realities-of-personnel-cuts/.

Lillis, Theresa. 2008. "Ethnography as Method, Methodology, and 'Deep Theorizing': Closing the Gap between Text and Context in Academic Writing Research." *Written Communication* 25 (3): 353–88.

Luebke, Steven R. 2002. "Using Linked Courses in the General Education Curriculum." *Academic Writing: Interdisciplinary Perspectives on Communication across the Curriculum* 3 (8). http://wac.colostate.edu/aw/articles/luebke_2002.htm.

Luken, Paul C., and Suzanne Vaughan. 2005. "'. . . Be a Genuine Homemaker in Your Own Home': Gender and Familial Relations in State Housing Practices, 1917–1922." *Social Forces* 83 (4): 1603–25.

Macrorie, Ken. 1988. *The I-Search Paper*. Portsmouth, NH: Heinemann.

Manning, Ambrose N. 1961. "The Present Status of the Research Paper in Freshman English: A National Survey." *College Composition and Communication* 12 (2): 73–78.

Marshall, Margaret. 2003. *Response to Reform: Composition and the Professionalization of Teaching*. Carbondale: Southern Illinois University Press.

Martins, David S. 2015. "Transnational Writing Program Administration: An Introduction," in *Transnational Writing Program Administration*, ed. David S. Martins, 1–18. Logan: Utah State University Press.

Marx, Karl. 1970. *A Contribution to the Critique of Political Economy (1859)*. Trans. S. W. Ryazanskaya. Ed. Maurice Dobb. New York: International.

Mazziotti, Donna, and Teresa Grettano. 2011. "'Hanging Together': Collaboration between Information Literacy and Writing Programs Based on the ACRL Standards and the WPA Outcomes." In *Declaration of Interdependence: The Proceedings of the ACRL 2011 Conference*, ed. Dawn Mueller, 180–90. Chicago: Association of College and Research Libraries.

McComiskey, Bruce. 2006. *English Studies: An Introduction to the Discipline(s)*. Chicago: National Council of Teachers of English.

McGuinness, Claire. 2006. "What Faculty Think: Exploring the Barriers to Information Literacy Development in Undergraduate Education." *Journal of Academic Librarianship* 32 (6): 573–82.

Miley, Michelle. 2017. "Looking Up: Mapping Writing Center Work through Institutional Ethnography." *Writing Center Journal* 36 (1): 103–29.

Miller, Susan. 1993. *Textual Carnivals: The Politics of Composition*. Carbondale: Southern Illinois University Press.

Mitchell, Michael, Michael Leachman, and Kathleen Masterson. 2016. "Funding Down, Tuition Up: State Cuts to Higher Education Threaten Quality and Affordability at Public Colleges." Center on Budget and Policy Priorities. August 5. https://www.cbpp.org/research/state-budget-and-tax/funding-down-tuition-up.

Moss, Beverly J. 1992. "Ethnography and Composition: Studying Language at Home." In *Methods and Methodology in Composition Research*, ed. Gesa Kirsch and Patricia A. Sullivan, 153–71. Carbondale: Southern Illinois University Press.

Murphy, Christina, and Byron Stay. 2012. *The Writing Center Director's Resource Book*. New York: Routledge.

Nader, Louise. 1972. "Up the Anthropologist: Perspectives Gained from 'Studying Up.'" In *Reinventing Anthropology*, ed. Del Hymes, 284–311. New York: Random House.

National Council of English Teachers. 2016. "An Update on NCTE Initiatives." March 15.

Nichols, Naomi, and Alison I. Griffith. 2009. "Talk, Texts, and Educational Action: An Institutional Ethnography of Policy in Practice." *Cambridge Journal of Education* 39 (2): 241–55.

North, Stephen M. 1987. *The Making of Knowledge in Composition: Portrait of an Emerging Field*. Portsmouth, NH: Heinemann.

Ohman, Richard. 1976. *English in America: A Radical View of the Profession*. New York: Oxford University Press.

Olson, Gary A., and Evelyn Ashton-Jones. 1988. "Writing Center Directors: The Search for Professional Status." *Writing Program Administration* 12: 19–28.

Pels, Dick. 2004. "Strange Standpoints, or How to Define the Situation for Situated Knowledge." In *Feminist Standpoint Theory Reader: Intellectual and Political Controversies*, ed. Sandra Harding, 273–90. New York: Routledge.

Perdue, Virginia. 1991. "Writing Center Faculty in Academia: Another Look at Our Institutional Status." *Writing Program Administration* 15 (1–2): 13–23.

Phelps, Louise Wetherbee. 1999. "Telling the Writing Program Its Own Story: A Tenth-Anniversary Speech." In *The Writing Program Administrator as Researcher: Inquiry in Action and Reflection*, ed. Shirley Rose and Irwin Weiser, 168–84. Portsmouth, NH: Boynton/Cook Heinemann.

Porter, James E., Patricia Sullivan, Stuart Blythe, Jeffrey T. Grabill, and Libby Miles. 2000. "Institutional Critique: A Rhetorical Methodology for Change." *College Composition and Communication* 51 (4): 610–42.

Rankin, Janet, and Marie Campbell. 2009. "Institutional Ethnography (IE), Nursing Work, and Hospital Reform: IE's Cautionary Analysis." *Forum Qualitative Sozialforschung / Forum: Qualitative Social Research* 10: n.p. http://www.qualitative-research.net/index.php/fqs/article/view/1258.

Ratcliffe, Krista. 1999. "Rhetorical Listening: A Trope for Interpretive Invention and a 'Code of Cross-Cultural Conduct.'" *College Composition and Communication* 52 (2): 195–224.

Raymond, James C. 1996. *English as a Discipline, or, Is There a Plot in This Play?* Tuscaloosa: University of Alabama Press.

Reiff, Mary Jo, Anis Bawarshi, Michelle Ballif, and Christian Weisser. 2015. *Ecologies of Writing Programs: Program Profiles in Context*. Anderson, SC: Parlor.

Rickly, Rebecca. 2008. "Messy Contexts: The Required Research Methods Course as a Scene of Rhetorical Practice." Writing Research across Borders Conference, University of California at Santa Barbara, February 22–24. http://www.writing.ucsb.edu/wrconf08/Pdf_Articles/Rickly_Article.pdf.

Rickly, Rebecca. 2012. "After Words: Postmethodological Musings." In *Writing Studies Research in Practice*, ed. Lee Nickoson and Mary P. Sheridan, 261–68. Carbondale: Southern Illinois University Press.

Russell, David R. 1991. *Writing in the Academic Disciplines, 1870–1990: A Curricular History*. 2nd ed. Carbondale: Southern Illinois University Press.

Saunders, Laura. 2012. "Faculty Perspectives on Information Literacy as a Student Learning Outcome." *Journal of Academic Librarianship* 38 (4): 226–36.

Schell, Eileen. 2003. "Materialist Feminism and Composition Studies: The Practice of Critique and Activism in an Age of Globalization." In *Fractured Feminisms: Rhetoric, Context, and Contestation*, ed. Laura Gray-Rosedale and Gil Harootunian, 31–43. Albany: State University of New York Press.

Schell, Eileen. 2012. "Materializing the Material as Progressive Research Method and Methodology." In *Practicing Research in Writing Studies: Reflexive and Ethically Responsible Research*, ed. Katrina M. Powell and Pam Takayoshi, 123–40. New York: Hampton.

Schilb, John. 2002. "The WPA and the Politics of LitComp." In *The Writing Program Administrator's Resource: A Guide to Reflective Institutional Practice*, ed. Stuart Brown, Theresa Enos, and Catherine Chaput, 165–79. Mahwah, NJ: Lawrence Erlbaum.

Scholes, Robert E. 1998. *The Rise and Fall of English: Reconstructing English as a Discipline*. New Haven, CT: Yale University Press.

Scott, Tony. 2009. *Dangerous Writing: Understanding and Political Economy of Composition*. Logan: Utah State University Press.

Scott, Tony, and Lil Brannon. 2013. "Democracy, Struggle, and the Praxis of Assessment." *College Composition and Communication* 65 (2): 273–98.

Shepley, Nathan. 2016. *Placing the History of College Writing: Stories from the Incomplete Archive*. Anderson, SC: Parlor. http://wac.colostate.edu/books/shepley/history.pdf.

Sheridan, Mary P. 2012. "Making Ethnography Our Own: Why and How Writing Studies Must Redefine Core Research Practices." In *Writing Studies Research in Practice: Methods and Methodologies*, ed. Lee Nickoson and Mary P. Sheridan, 73–85. Carbondale: Southern Illinois University Press.

Skinnell, Ryan. 2016. *Conceding Composition: A Crooked History of Composition's Institutional Fortunes*. Logan: Utah State University Press.

Smit, David W. 2004. *The End of Composition Studies*. Carbondale: Southern Illinois University Press.

Smith, Dorothy. 1974. "Women's Perspective as a Radical Critique of Sociology." *Sociological Inquiry* 44 (1): 7–13.

Smith, Dorothy. 2001. "Texts and the Ontology of Organizations and Institutions." *Studies in Cultures, Organizations, and Societies* 7 (2): 159–98.

Smith, Dorothy. 2002. "Institutional Ethnography." In *Qualitative Research in Action*, ed. Tim May, 17–52. Thousand Oaks, CA: Sage.

Smith, Dorothy. 2005. *Institutional Ethnography: A Sociology for People*. Walnut Creek, CA: Altamira.

Smith, Dorothy. 2006. *Institutional Ethnography as Practice*. New York: Rowman and Littlefield.

Smoot, Joyce. 1985. "Public Relations and the Writing Center Director: Making the Center Visible On and Off Campus." *Writing Lab Newsletter* 10 (1): 6–8.

Society for the Study of Social Problems. 2006. "Institutional Ethnography." *Social Problems* 53 (3): 293.

Soliday, Mary. 2002. *The Politics of Remediation: Institutional and Student Needs in Higher Education*. Pittsburgh: University of Pittsburgh Press.

Stinnett, Jerry. 2012. "Resituating Expertise: An Activity Theory Perspective on Representation in Critical Ethnography." *College English* 75 (2): 129–49.

Strauss, Anselm, and Juliet M. Corbin. 1997. *Grounded Theory in Practice*. New York: Sage.

Swales, John. 1990. *Genre Analysis: English in Academic and Research Settings*. Boston: Cambridge University Press.

Taggart, Amy Rupiper, H. Brooke Hessler, and Kurt Schick. "What Is Composition Pedagogy? An Introduction." In *A Guide to Composition Pedagogies*, ed. Gary Tate, Amy Rupiper Taggart, Kurt Schick, and H. Brooke Hessler, 1–19. New York: Oxford University Press.

Townsend, Elizabeth. 1996. "Institutional Ethnography: A Method for Showing How the Context Shapes Practice." *OTJR: Occupation, Participation, and Health* 16 (3): 179–99.

University of Washington College of Arts and Sciences. 2008. "College of Arts and Sciences Fact Sheet: English."

Wardle, Elizabeth. 2009. "'Mutt Genres' and the Goal of FYC: Can We Help Students Write the Genres of the University?" *College Composition and Communication* 60 (4): 765–89.

Welch, Nancy, and Tony Scott. 2016. *Composition in the Age of Austerity*. Boulder: University Press of Colorado.

Williams, Raymond. 1976. *Keywords: A Vocabulary of Culture and Society*. New York: Oxford University Press.

WPA Executive Committee. 1996. "Evaluating the Intellectual Work of Writing Program Administrators." *Writing Program Administration* 20 (1–2): 92–103. http://www.wpacouncil.org/positions/intellectualwork.html.

Wright, Ursula T., and Tonette S. Rocco. 2016. "Institutional Ethnography: A Holistic Approach to Understanding Systems." *International Journal of Adult Vocational Education and Technology* 7 (3): 27–41.

ABOUT THE AUTHOR

Dr. Michelle LaFrance directs the Writing across the Curriculum program at George Mason University. Michelle teaches graduate and undergraduate courses in writing course pedagogy, ethnography, and feminist/cultural materialist and qualitative research methodologies. She has published on peer review, preparing students to write across the curriculum, e-portfolios, e-research, writing center and WAC pedagogy, the material contexts of composition, and institutional ethnography. Her co-edited collection, *Peer Pressure/ Peer Power: Theory and Practice in Peer Review* (with Steven J. Corbett and Teagan Decker), was released by Fountainhead Press in 2014, and *Peer Review and Peer Response: A Critical Sourcebook* (with Steven J. Corbett) was released by Bedford St. Martin's in 2017. She is an avid home brewer, enjoys the outdoors, and attends live music shows as often as possible.

INDEX